The Guide To India

A Tibetan Account by Amdo Gendun Chöphel

Toni Huber

LIBRARY OF TIBETAN WORKS & ARCHIVES

First Print 2000

ISBN: 81-86470-25-5

Published by the Library of Tibetan Works and Archives, Dharamsala, H.P. 176215 India and printed at Indraprastha Press (CBT), New Delhi.

ཉེ་ཨོཾ་སྒྲ་བས་གཟེབ་ཏུ་རྫུད།།
འདབ་ཆགས་ལྷུགས་པ་བདེ་བར་ཀྲུ།།

In admiration of
the Amdo Beggar, and for all those
Tibetan pilgrims with whom I have
shared the road.

Contents

Illustrations

Preface

The present work contains the first complete English translation, together with Tibetan text edition, of the *rGya gar gyi gnas chen khag la 'grod pa'i lam yig*, Amdo Gendun Chöphel's modest but very popular pilgrim's or traveller's guide to India. In my Translator's Introduction, I have endeavored to place both the work and its composition carefully within the context in which they must be critically appreciated. However, much of the larger frame of reference which is very relevant here has been omitted or only briefly alluded to. I have not given treatment to the tradition of India as a Buddhist "holy land" for pilgrimage and the role this has played in Tibetan cultural and social life. Nor have I dealt with the longer history of Tibetan geographical writings and their representation of India as a Buddhist holy land to which Gendun Chöphel was heir. Instead, I have written on these important but barely studied topics separately and at length in another book, *The Holy Land Reborn. Pilgrimage and the Reinvention of Buddhist India in the Tibetan Tradition* (forthcoming). Similarly, the status of Gendun Chöphel's text as the first work of modern Tibetan literature, and the particular features allowing it to be described as "modern" have been dealt with in my article: "Colonial Archaeology, International Missionary Buddhism and the First Example of Modern Tibetan Literature", In *Bauddhavidyāsudhākaraḥ: Studies in Honour of Heinz Bechert on the Occasion of His 65th Birthday*. (Eds.) Petra Kieffer-Pülz & Jens-Uwe Hartmann,

Swisttal-Odendorf, Indica et Tibetica Verlag, 1997 (Indica et Tibetica, 30), pp. 297-318. Accordingly, I have given minimal attention to these issues herein. Interested readers are encouraged to consult these other works for further details.

I wish to thank Heather Stoddard and Michael Balk who kindly supplied different published versions of the Tibetan text. Gene Smith, Don Lopez, Dan Martin, and David Templeman generously supplied me with copies of works from their private collections. Per Kvaerne, Imgard Mengele, and David Templeman all gave me pre-publication versions of their own research to review. Rinzin Thargyal and Ngawang Thogme both helped to clarify several obscure passages in the Tibetan text. The staff of the Library of Tibetan Works and Archives in Dharamsala originally requested I produce the present work, and their cooperation throughout the project was particularly appreciated, especially that of Lobsang Shastri, Pema Khangsar, Tsering Namgyal, Tenzin Sonam, and Tashi Tsering. I am grateful also to Jens-Uwe Hartmann, who gave me good suggestions and corrections for some of the material. I owe a debt to Barry Clark, whose well-placed interest in Gendun Chöphel's work rekindled my own. I am also grateful to the late Michael Aris for the timely gift of his excellent study of Jigme Lingpa's *Account of India to the South*. Both his suggestions and example inspired the production of the present work in various ways. Assistance from the Faculty of Humanities and Social Sciences at Victoria University aided the final preparation of this work. I thank Nigel Bond for his draughting and design skills.

It is somewhat gratifying that the first Tibetan text I ever obtained and attempted to read many years ago as an aspiring young scholar of Tibetan pilgrimage has now been critically presented here. I only hope that I myself have managed to faithfully reckon and represent the esteemed Amdo Beggar!

A note on the rendering of Tibetan in this work: Regret tably, there is still no standard or widely accepted scholarly system for representing the Tibetan language in romanized form according to its pronunciation. It is also difficult in many cases for non-specialists to pronounce Tibetan words rendered in transliteration according to their proper spellings. I have thus used my own simple phonetic equivalents for Tibetan names throughout the main body of the text and notes. The exception being that, following certain translated terms and expressions, book titles, and quoted passages, I have supplied correct written forms of Tibetan words within parentheses or in notes, according to the common Wylie (1959) system of romanization. Correct orthography for all Tibetan proper names is found within parentheses following entries in the index. While these are mostly written in plain text, all spellings for proper names used by Gendun Chöphel and found in the translation are distinguished using italics within parentheses following their entry in the index.

Toni Huber
Wellington, March 2000

Translator's Introduction

The Author

It is a reasonable speculation that after the great figures of the 13th and 14th Dalai Lamas, Amdo Gendun Chöphel is probably one of the most written about of modern Tibetans. He certainly enjoys the status of a modern culture hero of sorts among a generation of Tibetan intellectuals, both in Tibet itself and within the exile community. He is often admired by Western scholars for his keen interest in the world that lay beyond that of parochial Tibetan concerns, and for his sometimes iconoclastic stance or ironic humour. There is no doubt that he was one of the more creative and controversial Tibetan intellectuals of the 20th century, and as a consequence there are a number of excellent Tibetan and Western language studies of his life available.[1] However, his important and not insubstantial oeuvre[2] has only recently begun to be studied and appreciated by non-Tibetan readers.[3]

We are obliged to discuss Gendun Chöphel yet again since he was the author of the text translated herein, *A Guide-book for Travel to the Holy Places of India (rGya gar gyi gnas chen khag la 'grod pa'i lam yig)*, and henceforth referred to as the *Guide to India*.[4] By way of introduction, only a brief and somewhat impressionistic account of the main events of Gendun Chöphel's life will be given below. Following this, we will look in far more detail at his twelve-year period (1934-1946) of pilgrimage travels in late colonial India and Ceylon. It is these experiences and this milieu which inform us most about why and how he wrote and published his *Guide to India*. This material has received only cursory treatment in the biographies to date. By providing this detailed introduction, I hope to cast Gendun Chöphel's writing in a more complex light, and one which clearly demonstrates the great influence upon him of the modern, late colonial milieu he associated with during his sojourn in India.

i. A Biographical Sketch

Gendun Chöphel was born in 1903 in the Tibetan village of Shölphang, within the valley of Repkong Sermajong.[5] Repkong district is located in the east of the large Tibetan sub-ethnic region of Amdo or Domed (i.e. southern Qinghai and parts of southwest Gansu for the Chinese), which covers the north-eastern sector of the vast Tibetan plateau. Thus, in keeping with Tibetan naming practices, he often referred to himself in his writings as Domedpa- (the "One From Domed") or Amdo Gendun Chöphel. As a child he was named Alag Ditsa. His parents were followers of the Nyingmapa sect of Tibetan Buddhism, and while a young boy he was recognized as a reincarnate lama of that sect. However, he was not formally enthroned and instead he attended the local monasteries belonging to the dominant Gelukpa sect in Amdo for education. Here he became a monk, received his ordination name of Gendun Chöphel, and completed a standard course of basic study including such subjects as logic, epistemology, grammar, and philosophical debate. Around 1920, he went on to further study at the large and well-known Gelukpa monastery of Labrang Tashikyil, where he apparently excelled. During his stay at Tashikyil he had contacts with an American missionary, Marion Griebenow, who lived close to the monastery from 1921 to 1949. Griebenow became fluent in

Amdo Tibetan and was called Sherab Danpel by the local people of Labrang. For most young rural Tibetans in the early 20th century, sustained encounters with foreigners were extremely rare. It is very likely that the curious young Gendun Chöphel got some of his early ideas about, and fascination for the modern world outside of Tibet from the American missionary Griebenow.[6]

In 1927, Gendun Chöphel made the long journey from his native Amdo to the holy city of Lhasa in Central Tibet. There he began a course of higher Buddhist studies in the great Gelukpa monastery of Drepung on the outskirts of the city. While a member of the monastery's Gomang college he became a pupil of the renowned Amdo scholar Geshe Sherab Gyatso (c.1884-1968). Geshe Sherab and his brilliant but unorthodox student were to have a turbulent relationship together over the years.[7] Although Gendun Chöphel studied higher level philosophy and was a very formidable debater, he was a rather non-conformist student who had little interest in attending classes and monastic ceremonies. While in Lhasa, during 1934, he met the erudite and politically minded Indian Sanskrit scholar Rahul Sankrityayan (1893-1963). He then completely abandoned monastic life shortly before he could have taken the examination for the highest degree of Geshe, and instead joined the Indian pandit on his expedition in search of ancient Sanskrit manuscripts preserved in Tibetan libraries. In November of the same year he journeyed with Sankrityayan to northern India by way of Nepal. For the next twelve years, with the exception of a scholarly expedition to the Tsang region of Tibet with Sankrityayan in 1938, Gendun Chöphel remained in India and Ceylon. During this time he travelled the sub-continent extensively. He also spent long periods dwelling in the hill areas around the districts of Kulu in Himachal Pradesh and the Darjeeling-Kalimpong region between Bengal and Sikkim, the latter area being a standard route for intercourse between Central Tibet and India, and the base for various Tibetan intellectuals, traders and exiles.

Gendun Chöphel was a person of great intellectual ability. While in India and Ceylon, he mastered English, Hindi, Sanskrit and Pāli. Through various friends and contacts he was also exposed to a wide range of modern Indian and European intellectual culture and new scientific and political ideas. His personal habits were also changed by his new experiences and environment and, completely ceasing to maintain his monastic vows, he openly indulged his inclinations for liquor, smoking and intimate relations with women. The remarkably diverse contents of Gendun Chöphel's oeuvre bare ample testimony to his great curiosity, his life experiences, and his extensive scholarly and artistic activity during his time outside of Tibet. Besides the *Guide to India*, his main book-length compositions include his controversial refutation of Madhyamaka Buddhist philosophy *Nāgārjuna's Intention Adorned* (*Klu sgrub dgongs rgyan*), his *Treatise on Passion* (*'Dod pa'i bstan bcos*), being an entertaining Tibetan manual of erotic love based upon the *Kāma Sūtra*, and the *White Annals* (*Deb ther dkar po*) which is an original history of ancient imperial Tibet and the first Tibetan historical work to draw upon the unique Dunhuang manuscripts recovered in Central Asia by Aurel Stein and Paul Pelliot at the turn of the century.

During the mid-1940s, in the Darjeeling area, Gendun Chöphel had developed contacts with various progressive Tibetan political exiles who were forming a revolutionary party with an aim to reform and modernize traditional Tibet. In 1946 he finally returned to Lhasa, but was soon after imprisoned by the arch-conservative Tibetan authorities, on a trumped up charge of counterfeiting. However, it is certain his detention was motivated by the Tibetan elite's fears of his newly made progressive political connections, and perhaps more so by his out-spoken criticisms against the traditional government and monastic system and the jealousy of enemies he had made within it. He was finally released from prison in 1949, although his health and morale were so badly degraded he never recovered. He also never took up his pen again. He passed away in 1951, at 47 years of age. Gendun Chöphel was a man out of step with his own society, and for this he paid the ultimate price.

ii. The Pilgrimage Years

It was his friend, the gifted and cosmopolitan Rahul Sankrityayan, who initially guided Gendun Chöphel on a pilgrimage of north Indian Buddhist holy sites during the beginning of his stay in India. A rare glimpse of their shared journey during the winter of 1934-1935 was given by Sankrityayan in one of his later autobiographical writings:

> We arrived finally in India. The *geshé* [Gendun Chöphel], who was born in some remote valley of the Yellow River, was very moved by the idea of seeing the natal land of the Lord Buddha. The dream which he had nourished for such a long time finally realized itself. I took him with me to visit the holy places of Buddhism in India. Everywhere we went [...] he explained in verse the life of Śākyamuni and sketched the places.[8]

The aging pandit's fond reminiscences sound very positive, yet Gendun Chöphel's own description of his arrival and initial stay in India is rather less than enthusiastic:

> [Travelling] in a south-westerly direction through Nepal, we crossed over to Chandragiri and before long met up with the Indian railway. On the eighteenth day of the tenth Tibetan month of my

> thirty-second year [i.e. thirty-first year in Western reckoning, approximately December, 1934], I drank the waters of the Gangā and for the entire winter of that year I stayed in the city of Pāṭaliputra [i.e. Patna] and experienced a sadness which was like falling into the middle of a lake of vermin.[9]

The conflict between his urge to explore the outside world, including pilgrimage around the great sacred sites of India, and the longing for his distant homeland (*pha-yul*) was to remain deep in Gendun Chöphel's heart. This was poignantly expressed in a poem he wrote in English while still in India during 1941:

> My feet are wandering neath alien stars,
> My native land,—the road is far and long.
> Yet the same light of Venus and Mars
> Falls on the small green valley of Repkong.
>
> Repkong,—I left thee and my heart behind,
> My boyhood's dusty plays,—in far Tibet.
> Karma, that restless stallion made of wind,
> In tossing me; where will it land me yet?
>
> ...I've drunk of holy Ganga's glistening wave,
> I've sat beneath the sacred Bodhi tree,
> Whose leaves the wanderer's weary spirit lave.
> Thou sacred land of Ind, I honour thee,
> But, oh, that little valley of Repkong,
> The sylvian brook which flows that vale along.[10]

After his early introduction to Indian Buddhist sites in the company of the pandit, Gendun Chöphel set off on his own pilgrimage explorations. Between 1935 and 1939 he travelled extensively throughout the sub-continent in search of further ancient holy places and new sources of information, either alone or together with a Tibetan friend named Amdo Rahob Jigme.

He often resorted to the cheapest or simplest forms of transportation—the buffalo cart, rickshaw, third class rail, or on foot—and noted down the travel fares at each stage of his journey to reach places associated with Buddhism in India.[11] He also spent more than a year in Ceylon, visiting and later describing all its major Buddhist sites and religious history in detail in several of his writings. Not possessing proper travel documents, some of his journeys where only possible through the help of elite connections, such as his trip to Ceylon, which was facilitated by the private secretary of the Mahārāja of Sikkim.[12]

This then, was the field research upon which a good part of Gendun Chöphel's *Guide to India* is based. There are some well-founded doubts about the actual extent of his pilgrimage travels. Although he included a section on Southeast Asian Buddhist holy sites near the end of the *Guide to India*, it is certain he never actually visited these places himself. His accounts of each area are very brief, and contain telltale errors, such as his mistaken description of the great monument at Barabuḍur. It was probably rather his thoroughness as a scholar and his knowledge of the historical records of earlier Indian Buddhist visitors to places such as Java that prompted him to include these areas in the *Guide to India*, based upon the reports of others. Also, Gendun Chöphel gives a lengthy description of the Swat Valley, an area identified by Tibetans as the Tantric power place of Uḍḍiyāna and hence renowned in Tibet as a land of Tantric origins. However, his account is rather disconcerting. This section of the text is nothing but a pastiche of other, mostly unacknowledged, original Tibetan and Western accounts, and suggests that he did not in fact go anywhere other than the lower entrance to the valley, not far from the railhead.

His biographers tell us he travelled around India in the spirit of the mendicant. It is well-known among Tibetans that an important projection of Gendun Chöphel's own self-identity was as the "Amdo beggar" (*a-mdo sprang-po*). In his pilgrimage and travel writings he often referred to himself as the "astute beggar" (*sprang-po dpyod-ldan*) or the "cosmopolitan" (*rgyal-khams rig-pa*, lit. "one who knows the countries"). This latter epithet served well to distinguish himself from most of his fellow countrymen with more limited horizons back home, while his beggar or mendicant identity was based upon the reality of his life conditions. As all his biographers mention, for the most part during his 1930s travels he was chronically short of money, or without any at all. It is hard not to imagine Gendun Chöphel the pilgrim appearing as merely a diminutive (he was of slight build) and somewhat down-at-heel foreign Asian traveler, rather insignificant while passing through colonial India's burgeoning humanity. Yet his writings attest that all the while, beneath the surface, his intense and creative intellect keenly scrutinized and recorded all he saw and heard.

The model for this life-style is of course well established in Tibetan culture in the figure of the wandering Tantric yogin, an ideal which was itself entirely derived from the classical Indian matrix. The yogin's often humble and neglected outer appearance is thought to mask a highly realized practitioner actively working with the world around themselves to both attain and experience spiritual realization. The yogin in the Tibetan tradition, as typified by the beloved poet-saint Milarepa (1040-1123), also has a didactic role in which his experiences of insight into the nature of the world are passed on to others, frequently to ordinary lay people. One can not help but wonder whether Gendun Chöphel at times regarded or modeled himself in some form of this role, regardless of whether or not he ever actually engaged in any Tantric practice.[13] His interesting paintings of and poems about the archetypal Tibetan yogin Milarepa attest in part to his sympathy for this type of character, as opposed to the rule-bound and institutionalized monastic style which he clearly could never conform to and indeed openly rejected.[14] There is also, as can be appreciated throughout the *Guide to India*, a strong didactic aspect to Gendun Chöphel's writings in the way they are addressed to his fellow Tibetans.

The Tantric yogin, like Gendun Chöphel himself, is more than just an ordinary pilgrim inspired by simple faith. The yogin's career is characterized by special forms of wandering asceticism, such as the *caryā* phase of *saṃpannakrama* practice when they "enter into the action" (*spyod-pa la gshegs-pa* in Tibetan), journeying forth into the world. This is not (as it is often presented) "spontaneous" wandering, for the yogin engaged in the *caryā* phase will typically travel between and dwell specifically at the twenty-four Tantric power places (*pīṭha*) and eight cemeteries (*aṣṭa-śmaśāna*) of India which are well-known in the Tantric texts of both Śaivism and Buddhism.[15] Interestingly, an aspect of Gendun Chöphel's pilgrimage travel was devoted to just this activity. Thus, he included a section on the twenty-four Tantric power places in his *Guide to India*, and elsewhere recorded extensive notes on these sites.

The Ragra Tulku, Thetong Thubten Chödar, a personal disciple and biographer of Gendun Chöphel, gives us insights into this aspect of his pilgrim travels. According to Ragra's biography, after Gendun Chöphel learned Hindi, he not only travelled around the main holy places of the Buddha but attempted to identify many of the twenty-four Tantric sites mentioned in the *Saṃvaratantra* corpus—an influential higher level Tantric cycle in the Tibetan tradition. We know he was familiar with Butön Rinchen Drub's (1290-1364) important commentary on the *Saṃvaratantra* cycle which discusses these sites,[16] and also with early travel accounts of Tibetan yogins who had attempted to visit them in India.[17] There had long existed multiple Tibetan catalogues of these Indian Tantric sites, and an equally long tradition of debate and confusion regarding their exact identity and location. It was precisely this problem of Tibetan Buddhist intellectual history that Gendun Chöphel was responding to.[18] He investigated both the archaic and the new names for these places, and attempted to identify them with Indian cities or towns they might be close to or equated with. Then, he went in person to some of the reputed twenty-four Tantric sites in India, such as Kāmarūpa, Rāmeśvara, Kulūta and Uḍḍiyāna. At such places he met with Hindu sādhus (*hin-dhu'i sngags-pa*) engaged in forms of asceticism. He learned much from talking to them, and was thus able to offer his own identifications of some of the twenty-four Tantric sites in his writings and also translate into Tibetan a commentary on the *Saṃvaratantra* by Kṛṣṇācārya.[19]

Although Gendun Chöphel left us much in his various writings by way of information about the sites he visited, we know very little about his actual personal experiences of pilgrimage to holy places. It does appear from some of the evidence that for him pilgrimage was as much about satisfying scholarly curiosity as it was about encounters with the sacred and of worship. It is said by his Tibetan biographers that while traveling around various holy sites, he was always busy writing detailed descriptions of the many new things he saw. He also sketched and painted, drew maps, and copied ancient inscriptions to illustrate these scholarly travel notes (see figures 1-6). On the other hand, we also have glimpses of Gendun Chöphel the pilgrim as a deeply religious person. Another of his Tibetan biographers, Kirti Tulku, briefly reports an event occurring on pilgrimage which reveals this side to us. According to Kirti, the following episode was recorded by Gendun Chöphel in one of his unpublished works:

> Everywhere he went on pilgrimage in India, he made a good travel account. At a few holy places very great miracles occurred. From among them, [there is the time] he directly encountered the Karsha Phagpa [i.e. the image of Ārya Triloknāth in the Chandra-bhāga Valley] and burst out crying uncontrollably. As Gendun Chöphel cried, when he looked up through his tears, elixir came out from the body of the Kasha Phagpa, after which it was completely wet.[20]

Such accounts of miraculous images have always been the stock-in-trade of Tibetan pilgrimage literature. If Gendun Chöphel did in fact relate this incident, it tells us that he was every bit the traditional Tibetan pilgrim and in some respects not deeply converted to modern, rational observation at the complete expense of his faith. Unfortunately, the available sources have little else to say on such personal experiences, or on his period of pilgrimage in general.

Fig. 1. Gendun Chöphel's drawing of Buddha's bathing pool and the stone pillar at Bodh Gayā.

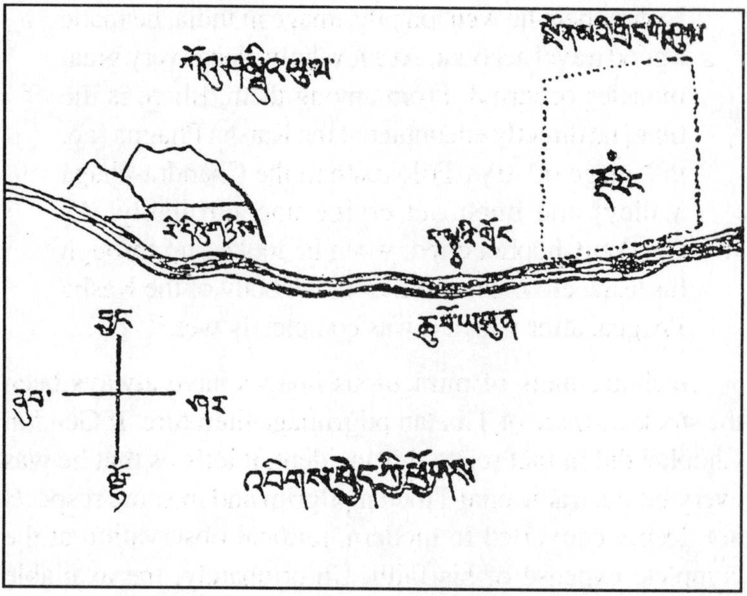

Fig. 2. Site plan of Kauśāmbī by Gendun Chöphel.

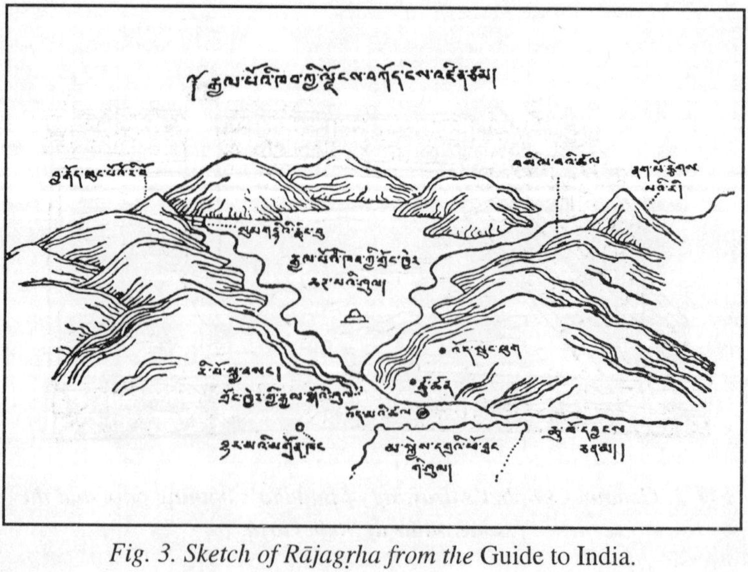

Fig. 3. Sketch of Rājagṛha from the Guide to India.

iii. Writing the Guide to India

The writing of the *Guide to India* was to take place over an extended period of time, and was heavily inspired by the particular cultural niche of 1930s India into which Gendun Chöphel entered and circulated. On the period of composition of the text, his biographies to date are confused,[21] although what he states in his own writings clearly shows the *Guide to India* was composed in three stages: An initial version in 1934/5 during his first pilgrimage; a more complete version in 1937, after undertaking further pilgrimage travels, and which was first published in 1939; and an expanded version in 1945/6 that was first published in 1950, and which is the one all later reprinted and edited versions have been based upon (see Appendix A).[22]

The composition of the *Guide to India* must also be appreciated in relation to his more extensive travel writing. A reputed result of this activity, two long manuscript works, known in his Tibetan biographies as the *Travel Account of India* (*rGya gar gnas yig*) and *Travel Account of Ceylon* (*Sing ga la'i gnas yig*) have yet to come to light in published form. However, his extensive work *The Golden Level: Tales of Wandering Around by a Cosmopolitan* (*rGyal khams rig pas bskor ba'i gtam rgyud gser gyi thang ma*), hereafter cited as *The Golden Level*, has now appeared in several editions.[23] He already began composing this work when he first met Rahul Sankrityayan and travelled with him through Central Tibet to India, and much of the content on certain topics is probably derived from Sankrityayan's erudite explanations to him of Indian classical culture and history.[24] *The Golden Level* contains seventeen chapters on a wide variety of subject matter informed by his pilgrimage travels, including essays on Indian place names, Aśokan inscriptions, trees and flowering plants of the sub-continent, the evolution of Indian and Tibetan scripts, royal lineages of the Gupta and Pāla dynasties, and Sinhalese history, to mention but a few. There is clearly a relationship between this work and the *Guide to India.* Many of the places and topics but briefly mentioned in the *Guide to India* are elaborated upon at length in *The Golden Level*, and the identical wording of passages is occasionally found in both works.

Why did Gendun Chöphel even write a guide-book to the Buddhist holy places of India? It is of course tempting just to assume that as an educated Tibetan Buddhist he would naturally be interested in Phagpaé Yül ('Phags-pa'i yul, Skt. Āryadeśa), the Indian Buddhist "holy land" which was traditionally revered as the fountainhead of Tibetan religious high culture. Yet, there is no biographical evidence that he maintained any strong earlier interests in the ancient Indian holy places of Buddhism or pilgrimage to them prior to meeting his influential friend Rahul Sankrityayan. On the other hand, there is every reason to think that Sankrityayan introduced him to all the inspiration he required in regard to such matters, not only by way of his personal example but crucially through the world of the Maha Bodhi Society of 1930s India. The extent to which Gendun Chöphel's involvement with the Maha Bodhi Society inspired and influenced the composition of his *Guide to India* and his other literary works should not at all be underestimated.[25] This important point has been neglected by his biographers, as has the active role the Maha Bodhi Society played in the revival of modern Buddhist pilgrimages to India in recent writing on Buddhism.[26]

At the time of his meeting with Gendun Chöphel in Tibet, Rahul Sankrityayan was actively engaged in the very quest which had led to the first real orientalist scholarship on the ancient Indian religion of Buddhism-the collection and study of old surviving Sanskrit manuscripts. Sankrityayan's own carrier and interests were perfectly suited to inspire his young Tibetan acquaintance in regard to pilgrimage in the modern, re-discovered Buddhist holy land and also in the art of guide-book writing. In 1920, the pandit had performed his own pilgrimage to the Indian Buddhist holy sites which the Maha Bodhi Society, of which he was an active member, had helped to restore. Afterwards he had composed a verse eulogy (*mahātmya*) of the main places connected with the life of the historical Buddha. Sankrityayan, under the name Baba Ramodar, was then active between 1922 and 1924 in the movement organized by the Maha Bodhi Society to legally reclaim the temple site of Bodh Gayā for Buddhist ownership.[27] After Sankrityayan initially guided Gendun Chöphel on a pilgrimage of north Indian Buddhist holy sites during the beginning of his stay in India, he introduced his Tibetan friend into the milieu of the Indian Maha Bodhi Society.[28]

The Maha Bodhi Society was founded in 1891 by one Don David Hēvāvitarana (1864-1933), a Sinhalese layman who took the name Dharmapāla, "Defender of the Dharma". Dharmapāla is without doubt one of the most remarkable figures in modern Buddhist history.[29] His legacy includes, amongst other things, the early establishment of Buddhism as a missionary religion in the modern world system, the raising of a new pan-Asian Buddhist consciousness, and the revival of Buddhist religious and historical sentiments about India as a holy land. While in India, Gendun Chöphel eventually joined and worked for the Maha Bodhi Society. It was in fact through the Calcutta headquarters of the Society, where he was employed for a time, that he got his *Guide to India* published in 1939. It is well known that Gendun Chöphel was disillusioned by what he saw as the heavily conservative and self-serving elite of his own Buddhist institutions and society in Tibet. In contrast to this, in India and Ceylon at the time of composing the *Guide to India*, he took the Buddhist Modernist activist Dharmapāla, the Maha Bodhi Society, and even some of the Theravāda monks with whom they were associated as a more positive model of what a socially engaged modern Buddhism could be like.[30]

It is clear that Gendun Chöphel was much impressed by the figure of Dharmapāla when he wrote the *Guide to India*. When offering his Tibetan readers a capsule biography of the activist, he refers to him as a "great soul" (mahātman) selflessly working for all Buddhists "by way of a hundred difficulties and without regard for life and property" (p.14). Dharmapāla's efforts to reestablish modern Buddhist centers at Sārnāth and elsewhere are described by his Tibetan admirer as "the beginnings of the later diffusion of the Buddhist teachings in India" (p.14). The use of the Tibetan historiographical term "later diffusion" (*phyi-dar*) here to invoke a parallel with the so-called later diffusion of Indian Buddhism to Tibet would certainly not have been lost on his educated Tibetan readers. Dharmapāla's works, and particularly the long-running campaign for repossession of the contested site of Bodh Gayā, are described sincerely by Gendun Chöphel several times in the course of the *Guide to India*.

Whatever Gendun Chöphel may have thought of Dharmapāla, we should not forget that right from the beginning of his visit to India, he entered into and maintained close contacts with the missionary milieu of the Maha Bodhi Society's modern pilgrimage industry, a development which reached its peak in the 1930s and early 1940s. The Society was active in heavily promoting the revival of ancient Buddhist sites such as Bodh Gayā and Sārnāth by encouraging the renewal of international pilgrimage to them. This whole revival process was intimately linked both to Dharmapāla's ongoing legal and political campaign to return the control of Bodh Gayā from Hindu to Buddhist hands, and the pan-Asian and global missionizing strategies for spreading the Society's brand of Buddhist Modernism. Since Gendun Chöphel enjoyed full access to the mass of existing Maha Bodhi Society publications promoting Buddhist pilgrimage to India, it is no surprise to find extensive evidence of their influence and adaptation throughout the *Guide to India*. The style of his descriptive content and itinerary in places, the extensive references to the railway network (including his railway map),[31] the citation of the Chinese pilgrim's accounts, and even the leading quotations of passages on pilgrimage from the *Mahāparinirvāṇa-sūtra* were all standard features of a host of earlier Maha Bodhi Society publications of the day.[32] To cap it all off, the *Guide to India* even closes with an outline of the Maha Bodhi Society's "good works" and a missionary appeal for support directed towards potential Tibetan members and patrons.

Finally, the possibility should be seriously considered that the Maha Bodhi Society itself, or one of its active members, actually requested Gendun Chöphel to compose the *Guide to India* for its missionary publications program. It clearly would have suited the Society's aims to have its message extended north over the Himalayas to a Tibetan Buddhist readership in this manner. Here we can cite a message read to the Maha Bodhi Society (and later published in their journal *The Maha Bodhi*) on the occasion of the opening of its Mūlagandhakuṭī Vihāra at Sārnāth in 1931, and composed by Lama Yongden, the cosmopolitan Sikkimese monk who was the companion-servant (and later adopted son) of the well-known French Tibetologue Alexander David-Neel (1868-1969). The message reads like a modern Tibetan "prophecy" concerning the composition of the *Guide to India*:

> Each winter numbers of Tibetan pilgrims come down from their high land to visit the Buddhist sacred places which are well known to them. It is most probable that some of my countrymen, either belonging to the Sangha or lay men, will be present at

> the opening of the Mulagandhakuti Vihāra. They will be well aware that this is the place where the Buddha preached his first sermon and will be glad to see a beautiful vihāra newly built on that holy spot. Yet, one may fear that they will not clearly understand to whom we are indebted for its achievement! Had I been happy enough to be present at the function I would have explained it at length to them, in Tibetan language. As this is not possible I wish that others tell them, in details...so that they can make it known all over Tibet as a good and inspiring example.[33]

One can but wonder whether Gendun Chöphel himself read this very message some years later and answered the call? We do know his *Guide to India* was indeed successful as missionary propaganda among Tibetans. In Lhasa during the 1940s, its Tibetan readers came across the Maha Bodhi Society appeal written at the end of the work and immediately sought to subscribe as members.[34] Another more likely source of inspiration for Gendun Chöphel to write, publish, and then later also revise the *Guide to India* was the ethnic Tibetan Christian missionary, Khunu Tharchin (1890-1976). Tharchin resided in Kalimpong and edited and published the first Tibetan newspaper, the *Melong*, and many other Tibetan language publications.[35] Kalimpong, the conduit for much of the political, economic and religious traffic between India and Tibet during the period, became an important base for Gendun Chöphel during his stay in India. It was there, before he wrote the *Guide to India*, that he met Tharchin who began to publish various of his writings, such as poems and small articles. Afterwards, in the 1940s, Tharchin was well-known for giving aid to Tibetan pilgrims en route to the Indian Buddhist holy places by printing leaflets and maps to assist them and allowing them to stay at a warehouse across the street from his press.[36]

As a product of all these influences, the writing of Gendun Chöphel's *Guide to India* was just one part of a large and complex socio-religious movement taking place at the time; a unique movement led by and consisting of a truly international cast of modern Buddhists all focused upon the revived Indian holy land. Yet, Gendun Chöphel did have his own strong Tibetan background and agenda with which to interpret and utilize such influences, and these are very evident in the *Guide to India*. He was writing for a Tibetan pilgrim audience who still carried much of the traditional cultural baggage about India which had began accumulating after the 13th century loss of the Buddhist holy land, and he wanted to address these deeply ingrained attitudes and ideas using his newly gained modern knowledge.

The Book

Although other early 20th century Tibetan travel accounts of India were written, Gendun Chöphel's work was the only systematic guide-book composed before the 1950s.[37] At the time it first appeared in 1939, it represented a marked departure from the way traditional Tibetans had come to consider India during the course of preceding centuries. In addition, when propagated in its original published form, it was one of the very first examples of modern native Tibetan literature.[38] Some of the features which define it as "modern" are: Its synthetic and critical approach to providing an up to date Buddhist historical geography of Indian sites; its functional guide for visiting them using modern means of transportation; and its inclusion of some of the first examples of modern Tibetan cartography which Gendun Chöphel himself drew (see figures 4-7).

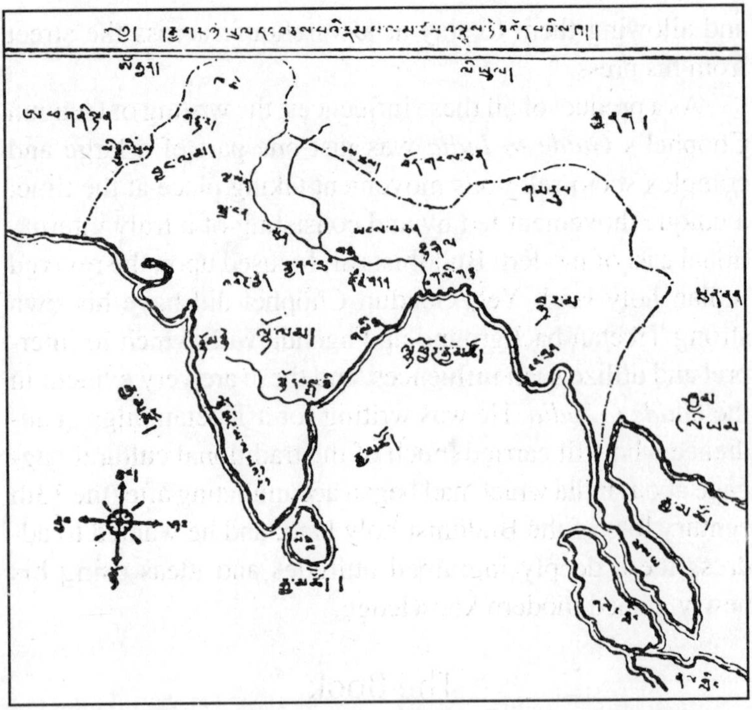

Fig. 4. Map of India and surrounding countries from the Guide to India.

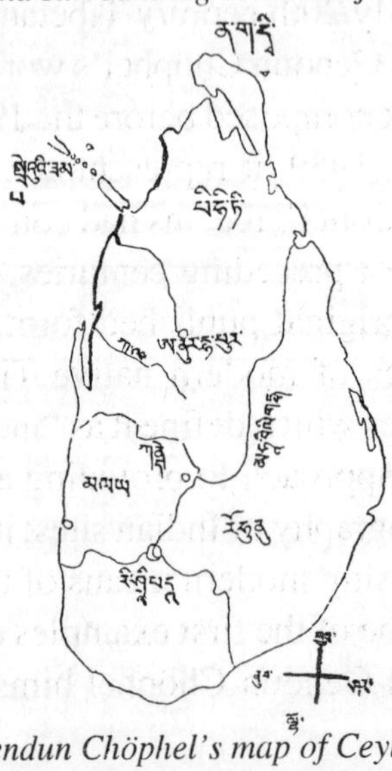

Fig. 5. Gendun Chöphel's map of Ceylon.

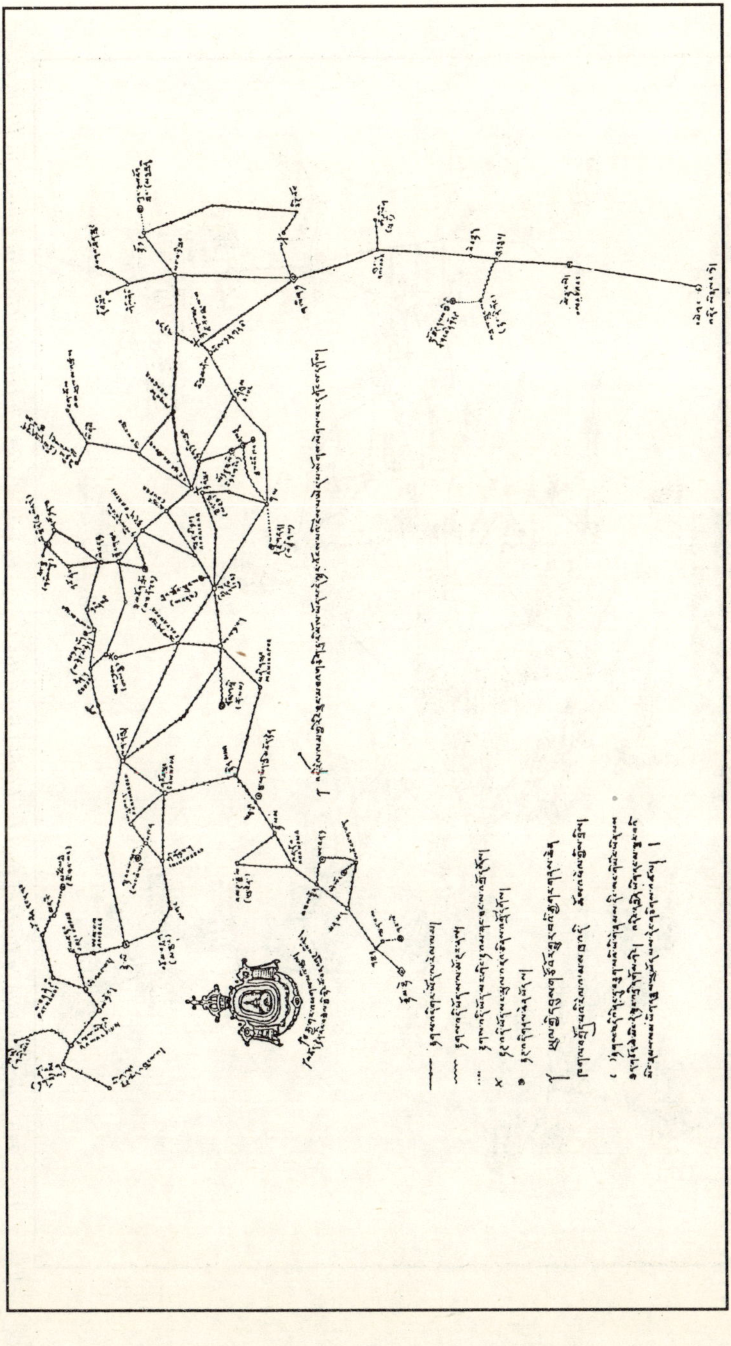

Fig. 6. Tibetan pilgrimage map of the Indian rail system from the Guide to India.

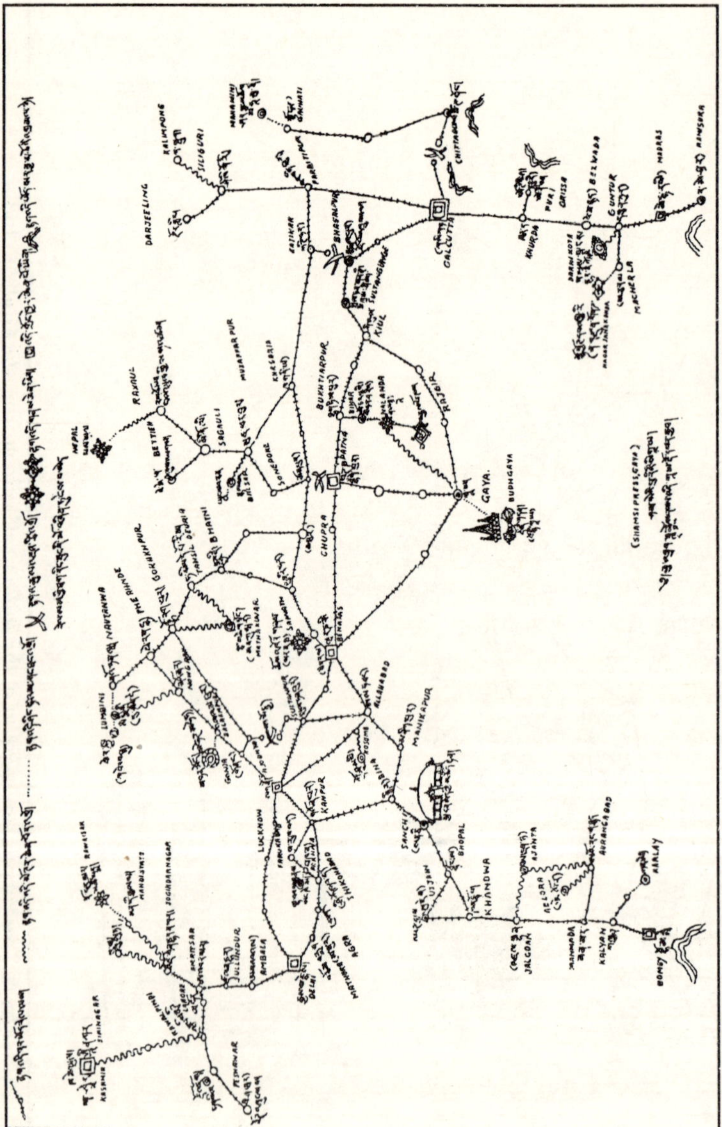

Fig. 7. 1952 Tibetan pilgrimage map of India adapted from the Guide to India, *and sold at the Tibetan temple in Bodh Gayā.*

Gendun Chöphel wrote his guide to India at a time when Tibetans had just begun to return in large numbers to their Buddhist holy land as pilgrims. This had been made possible due to the late 19th- and early 20th century rediscovery by colonial archaeologists of the neglected or burried Buddhist cult sites associated with the life of the historical Buddha, and the religious revival of these same sites which followed rapidly after thanks chiefly to the works of modern Buddhist missionary groups like the Maha Bodhi Society. This revival came after centuries during which the Tibetans had no or little access to India for religious travel, and during which, with great cultural inventiveness, they had constructed their own alternative religious geography of the sub-continent as a substitute for the lost original Buddhist cult places.[39] Many of the sites traditional Tibetans came to accept as connected with the Buddha or with their Buddhist history were clearly spurious from the point of view of 20th century scholarship in archaeology, philology and history. Two brief examples should suffice to illustrate this point. Firstly, although the historical Buddha Śākyamuni died and attained final *nirvāṇa* at the site of Kuśinagarī located at Kasia in the present-day Deoria District of south-eastern Uttar Pradesh, Tibetan Buddhists have, since at least the late 16th century, relocated this major Buddhist holy place as being some 500 kilometers to the east in central Assam, at an obscure spot called Hājo near the town of Gauhāti. Since its "discovery" by Tibetan lamas, great numbers of faithful pilgrims have visited the spot over the centuries in order to worship there, blissfully ignorant of its pure inventedness.[40] Secondly, we have the example of the Golden Temple, the principal shrine of the Sikh religion in Amritsar. Bonpo pilgrims in India earlier this century accepted the site as Gyalkhar Bachö, the palace of the ancient sage Milü Samleg who revealed the Bonpo Mother Tantras (*Magyü*), and whose secret name was held to be Guru Nanak.[41]

This unique interpretation of Sikhism and its holiest shrine enjoyed quite wide popularity among Tibetan Bonpos. For their part, early 20th century Tibetan Buddhists identified the holy tank surrounding the Sikh's Golden Temple in Amritsar as the sacred lotus lake associated with their important saint Padmasambhava, and it became a most popular place of pilgrimage for them.[42]

There have always been two main schools of thought among Tibetan scholars concerning their own traditions of religious geography. The more common position is to uncritically accept all sorts of claims, revelations and discoveries related to the identity of new holy places without regard to history and sometimes with little concession to common sense. The other minority position is that of the sceptics who tended to reject new claims of religious geography unless they conformed in terms of proper scripture and reasoning. Well-known figures of this latter type include the Sakya Pandita, Kunga Gyaltsen (1182-1251), the Fourth Khamtrül, Tenzin Chökyi Nyima (1730-1779), and the Tsenpo Nomonhan, Jampé Chökyi Tenzin Trinley (1789-1838). Gendun Chöphel was to join the ranks of this critical school of thought when he wrote his *Guide to India*. However, he rose above the traditional sectarianism which fuelled and coloured many earlier writings, and instead addressed his criticisms universally to all Tibetans as pilgrims in India.

The strong tendency on the part of Tibetan pilgrims from all backgrounds to speculate about the location and identity of Indian holy sites was a great bane for Gendun Chöphel, and one he directly and most critically addressed throughout his *Guide to India*. Geographical ignorance was a theme which was also to occupy him in several of his other works. For example, he argued vigorously against the traditional Tibetan "flat earth theory" in his article *Is the World Round or Flat*? (*'Jig rten ril mo 'am zlum po*?) published in 1938 in the

Kalimpong based Tibetan language newspaper *Melong*.[43] However, in spite of Gendun Chöphel's repeated pronouncements in the *Guide to India* of providing an entirely accurate and new presentation of holy India to the Tibetan public, his work is itself populated by his own unique interpretations of Buddhist historical geography, fantastic stories and outright errors (these are all discussed in the Notes to the Translation). This is so for even the most fundamental of Buddhist traditions. To give but one typical example: In the opening pages of the *Guide to India* he lists the eight important sites in the Buddha's life and the eight great *stūpa* located at them (*aṣṭamahāsthānacaitya*) to which devout Buddhists could make pilgrimages with the promise of obtaining better rebirths. However, in a departure from both the classical Buddhist literary and popularly accepted *aṣṭamahāsthānacaitya* scheme he inexplicably replaces the name of Vaiśālī with that of Nālandā.[44]

The over-confident tone along with the factual errors in the *Guide to India* raised the ire of at least one Tibetan scholar, being none other than Gendun Chöphel's own former teacher Geshe Sherab Gyatso, with whom he had a most turbulent relationship, at times leading even to the point of physical violence between them.[45] Sherab Gyatso wrote an interesting critique of the *Guide to India*, beginning with the remark "In this little pilgrimage guide-book for India there are many defects."[46] For example, he pointed out, quite correctly, Gendun Chöphel's erroneous time reckoning relating to the birth of the founder of Sikhism, Guru Nanak (1469-1539), by stating:

> [Gendun Chöphel] wrote: "Guru Nanak Deva was born in the earth-ox [year] of the eighth calendrical cycle, and up to this present [year] of the fire-ox [=1937] six hundred and four years have elapsed." [I] take this to be utterly wrong. The duration up to

> that [year] was not six hundred and four years, it was no more than four hundred and sixty nine [years]... By stating "six hundred and four [years]" he gives the impression of very detailed precision... still more, he says: "One need not have even a shred of doubt [about my accuracy]." The complete contradiction within this guide-book is just a source of senseless worry for some confused pilgrims.[47]

Despite its anomalies and the criticism these received, the *Guide to India* deserves to be credited as one of the most accurate and well-informed accounts of Buddhist India available in Tibetan language until recent times. We must also consider that the author's over-confident tone in places was probably also for stylistic reasons, and intended to amuse his Tibetan readers.

The *Guide to India* has continued to circulate and have relevance for Tibetans as both pilgrims and exiles in India up until the present-day. During the 1980s and early 1990s I found copies of it in the possession of Tibetan pilgrims I interviewed at various Indian Buddhist sites, and many Tibetan exiles I have talked to either owned a copy, or have read it or heard about it. The now old and battered 1984 reprint copy I first obtained in India some 15 years ago is prefaced by a short editorial statement in Tibetan explaining that the book was reissued due to the demand created by a great increase in the numbers of Tibetan pilgrims visiting Indian Buddhist sites. And as a testimony to its popularity and utility, it has appeared in over a dozen reprinted and edited versions, as well as inspiring other modern works (see Appendix A). Because Gendun Chöphel's *Guide to India* offered a new and critical representation of India which became widespread, it is an important source when considering changing Tibetan visions of the Buddhist holy land, not to mention attitudes towards India and pilgrimages there shaped by Buddhist Modernism.

Remarks on the Edition and Translation

There have been previous unfulfilled efforts to publish a translation of the *Guide to India*. The renowned Tibetologist Ariane Macdonald (née Spanien) signaled a complete French translation, together with a biographical introduction on Gendun Chöphel, as "en préparation" in 1970, although it never appeared in press.[48] She was, however, one of the first scholars to use the *Guide to India* in published research—D. K. Barua being the first[49]—and she translated several short passages into French.[50] Some years ago, a flawed and partial English draft of a poorly edited Tibetan exile reprinting of the text was also produced by Barry Clark, a Western practitioner of Tibetan medicine based in Dharamsala. In addition, the doyen of Tibetan pilgrimage studies, Alexander Macdonald, translated some 3-4 pages of the heavily edited 1968 Dalhousie version of the *Guide to India* into English, although he himself rightly recognized these were the insertions of a later editor.[51] Gendun Chöphel's principal Western biographer, Heather Stoddard, also translated several short passages from the 1950 Gangtok version into French.[52] I also know of several other Tibetologists who have old draft translations of the *Guide to India* gathering dust in their files or tucked away in the memory of their computers.

The present translation is based upon my edition of the now rare Gangtok (Sikkim Government Press, 1950) printing of the final expanded 1945 version of the *Guide to India*. In no instance do any of the later edited and reprinted versions offer better readings. The 1950 print is remarkably free of errors. My emendations have the original readings (= *orig.*) supplied in footnotes. Non-Tibetan devices used in the original print have been retained, including: ( ), =, —, -:, underlining, and Roman script in UPPER and plain lower case. The exception is Devanāgarī script, which I have represented in Roman *italics*. Pagination is shown in brackets. Note that no number appears for page 11 in either the edition or translation as it carries an illustration in the original.

As the *Guide to India* contains a great many proper names in various languages and scripts, I have resorted to the following system for representing them in the parallel translation to follow. Most classical Indian names for historical sites and persons are given in their Sanskrit spellings (or common variants thereof), regardless of whether they are Gendun Chöphel's Tibetan translations (e.g. rTsa-mchog-grong for Kuśinagarī), transliterations (e.g. Ajātashatru for Ajātaśatru) or phonetic transcriptions (e.g. Shang-kha-sa for Sāṃkāśya). Certain names, where appropriate, are given in their Pāli forms, for the author was also well versed in that language. For most modern Indian place names, I have followed the standard official spellings of the *National Atlas of India* (1979). Every original Tibetan spelling of proper names used by Gendun Chöphel can be found in the index. These are rendered in the Wylie (1959) system of transliteration, written in italics, and placed within parentheses following each index entry. In order to aid his readers in the practical use of his text, Gendun Chöphel also used underlining for important place names and, in particular for railway station names, he employed upper case Roman script mostly together with a Tibetan phonetic pronunciation guide (e.g. <u>Mo-ja-phar-pur</u> MUZAFFARPUR). These devices have all been preserved in the translation. In the section on Tantric sites he also supplied the Devanāgarī equivalent for some names, and these are given in italics (e.g. Nagara=*Śrīnagara*). Both my own significant clarifying additions in the translation, and the original pagination are shown within brackets. Dates, where known, for historical persons are supplied within parentheses following the first occurrence of the name.

Notes to Translator's Introduction

1. See Dejin Zangmo (1978), Karmay (1980), Dhondup (1978), Stoddard (1985a, 1985b, 1988), Ruegg (1989), Hopkins & Yuthok (1992:11-31), Rakra Thetong (1992), Lopez (1995), Bogin & Decleer (1997), and Mengele (1999). For readers of Tibetan see [gZhis-rtse] Ri-kha (1972), Bla-chung A-pho (1973), Rak-ra (1980), Hor-khang (1983), Kirti (1983), Zam-gdong-pa (1986), Khang-dkar (1992), Nor-brang O-rgyan (1995), and rDo-rje-rgyal (1997).
2. Different lists of Gendun Chöphel's published, unpublished and attributed works can be found in Dhondup (1978:18), Kirti (1983:44-48), Stoddard (1985a:329-336) and Hor-khang (1990, vol.3:541-544). These lists have now been systematically treated and updated by Mengele (1999:chapt. 4).
3. Gendun Chöphel's literary output can be divided into three categories: original written works; translations; collaborations. Concerning only the first category, to date just two fully translated versions of his longer original works have been published: the *White Annals* (*Deb ther dkar po*) into English (problematic translation by Norboo 1978; review by Richardson 1978); and the *Treatise on Passion* (*'Dod pa'i bstan bcos*) also into English (by Hopkins & Yuthok 1992). A few brief passages have been translated from *Nāgārjuna's Intention Adorned* (*Klu sgrub dgongs rgyan*) into English (by Lopez 1994a, 1994b, who is also preparing for publication a complete translation and study of this important work). A short newspaper article entitled "The Evolution of dBu-med from dBu-can [Tibetan Script]" (*dBu can las dbu med rang byung du grub pa*) was translated into English (by Dhondup 1983, see also Narkyid 1982). Concerning the second category of works, an English translation has been made of Gendun Chöphel's original Tibetan translation of the Pāli *Dhammapada* (see dGe-'dun Chos-'phel 1985).
4. See Appendix A for full bibliographical details. Although others have rendered Tibetan *lam-yig* variously with "travel notes", "passport",

"itinerary" or "route description", etc., I translate it with "guide" or "guide-book" on account of the obvious intent of the contents in this case (cf. Large-Blondeau 1960:213); on the danger of defining genres in relation to such very fluid Tibetan terms, see Decleer (1998:73-75).

5. His birth year has been problematic, given as either 1894/5, 1902, 1903 or 1905 in various sources, see Ruegg (1989:307-8) and Zamgdong-pa (1986:12-13). Some time ago A. Macdonald (1970:204) already gave the correct birth year, and van der Kuijp (1996:49, n.2) finally clarified the issue with reference to Gendun Chöphel's own writings.
6. On Griebenow's life in Tibet see Nietupski (1999).
7. On Geshe Sherab Gyatso see Phun-tshogs (1998); and on the relationship between Gendun Chöphel and Geshe Sherab Gyatso see Stoddard (1988), Khang-dkar (1992).
8. Quoted from R. Sankrityayan, 1957. *Jinkā maiṁ kṛtagya*. Ilahabad, Kitab Mahal, p.208, as cited in Stoddard (1985a:172), my translation from the French.
9. *gTam-rgyud* 1:40.
10. Anon (1941:294-295).
11. Stoddard (1985a:185).
12. Dhondup (1978:13).
13. Gendun Chöphel has already been generally compared to Milarepa, and also to the figure of the "saintly madman" (*smyon-pa*), the bodhisattva, and various other cultural stereotypes by his biographers. My concern here is only to consider, in relation to the available information, how he might have felt about himself while on pilgrimage.
14. See for example his painting of the saint in Hor-khang (1990:frontispiece to vol.3), and his English poems "Melareppa's Reply" and "Manassarowar" in Anon (1941:293, 295).
15. It is now well established that the Buddhist Yoginī-tantra texts through which the Tibetans obtained these traditions derived much of their content directly from Śaiva sources, including the cult of the *pīṭha* (Sanderson 1990, 1994). On the tradition of wandering to Indian Tantric sites according to Tibetan Buddhist sources, see Huber (1990), Templeman (1999) and Tucci (1940).
16. For this work see Bu-ston (1966), pp.1-118.
17. For example, he cites use of accounts by Orgyenpa Rinchenpal (1230-1308/9) and Tagtsang Repa Ngawang Gyatso (1574-1651); on which see Tucci (1940).

18. For a listing and analysis of Tibetan literary sources concerning this historical debate see Huber (1990).
19. Rak-ra (1980:50-53).
20. Kirti (1983:100). A Tibetan interpretation of the site of Triloknāth, in a guide-book entitled *Ras 'phags 'phags pa'i gnas bshad*, with an account of the miraculous image, is found in Schubert (1935a).
21. Dhondup (1978:18) states only that he wrote it in Ceylon after his Indian pilgrimages. According to Stoddard that would have been either in 1937 or again in 1939-1940 (1985a:180, 343). In two different statements Stoddard gives both 1937 and 1938, without noting a source for these datings (1985a:185, 330).
22. Gendun Chöphel states in the final 1945/6 version of the *Guide to India*, for the 1934 date: "I myself wrote this guide-book in India over twelve years ago" (p.46); in the body of the text he states he writes in "this present fire-ox [year of the Tibetan calendar=1937]" (p.15); and several times he states that since the Buddha's *parinirvāṇa* "two thousand four hundred and eighty nine years have elapsed" (pp.1, 47). He claimed to have adopted the Theravāda Buddhist dating system after visiting Ceylon, although he was not always consistent about using it. We know he calculated from the year 555 B.C.E. while he was writing in 1946 to date that year as 2490 after Buddha's *parinirvāṇa* (dGe-'dun Chos-'phel 1990a:238), and therefore his 2489 for 1945/6 appears to be in general agreement with the rest of the time frame he provided. His dates are internally consistent, regardless of whether they conform to any accepted version of the Theravāda dating system. Concerning the revised and expanded final version of 1945/6, his personal student Hor-khang (1990, vol.3:542) states: "An expanded version of the small *Guide-book for Travel to the Holy Places of India* was composed by him in the year 1945." This version was first printed in Gangtok in 1950, but still with the original 1939 front cover, which appears to have confused some later readers concerning the date of its composition (e.g. A. Macdonald 1970:204, n.2).
23. The full version is published in *gTam-rgyud*, while dGe-'dun Chos-'phel (1986) contains only the first chapter, a chapter title list and a few verses.
24. Hor-khang (1990:3).
25. A good example of this is his translation from Pāli into Tibetan of the *Dhammapada*. Apart from the *Dhammapada*'s historical absence from the Tibetan Buddhist canon, that he choose to translate this text was no doubt strongly influenced by the fact that it was the focus of

a modern Buddhist translation program under the auspices of the Maha Bodhi Society during the 1930s. The Sankrityayan connection surfaces here yet again, for in 1938 the pandit also published a Hindi version of the *Dhammapada* together with the original Sanskrit and Pāli texts as part of the Society's *Dhammapada* translation and publication program, a program which helped establish the *Dhammapada* as the single most translated Buddhist scripture in history. The Maha Bodhi Society also published a number of other translations of the work into Indian languages during the 1930s. For the *Dhammapada*, according to a recent reckoning, there are no less than 100 translations into European languages, 73 translations into Indian languages and 43 translations into other Asian languages (including Arabic); see Hecker (1993).

26. For example, a scholarly survey of Buddhism widely used in university teaching only states that the 20th century increase in Buddhist pilgrimage to India is "...due largely to the availability of modern transportation, the relative stability of Indian politics, and the health of the Asian economy" (Robinson & Johnson 1997:50).
27. Stoddard (1985a:158).
28. Stoddard (1985a:185).
29. On Dharmapāla see, in particular, Bechert (1966), Dharmapala (1965), Bechert (1984), Gombrich (1988) and Gombrich & Obeyesekere (1988).
30. It is reported he was also highly impressed by Theravāda monks he met with in Ceylon (Dhondup 1978:13; Mengele 1999:57-58). He suggested modern reforms of the Tibetan monastic system, advocating the monks be given salaries instead of agricultural estates for their support, and that they be forbidden to engage in business and required to study instead (Goldstein 1989:453).
31. Concerning his map, the interesting precursor is the *Buddhist Pilgrim's Railway Guide Map for India*, published in Rangoon by the Publicity Department of the Burma Buddhist Pilgrim's Agency in 1928. The map also included advice to pilgrims traveling to India and, like the *Guide to India*, another small outline map of Buddhist India; see Anon (1928:230). Gendun Chöphel's original 1939 rail map (see figure 6 of the present work) later served as the basis for several other redrawn versions (artists unknown). One dated 1952 (*chu-'brug-lo*) and printed at the Shamsi Press, Gayā, was sold to pilgrims at the Tibetan temple in Bodh Gayā during the 1950s (see figure 7 of the present work). For comments on its use by Tibetan pilgrims see Large-Blondeau (1960:216, 219). This later, redrawn

map was reproduced by Stoddard (1985a:Carte IV) and incorrectly cited as being "publiée dans le Lamyig". A second and cruder re-drawn version appears, printed upside down, in the heavily edited 1968 Dalhousie edition of the *Guide to India*.

32. Publication of articles concerning pilgrimage to the archeologically recovered Buddhist sites of India in the Maha Bodhi Society's journal, *The Maha-Bodhi*, was already part of the Society's activities at the turn of the century. See, for example, Saddhananda (1898), Anon (1898a), Anon (1899) and, in particular, Chandrima (1902) whose article on the four main sites associated with the Buddha's biography provides prospective pilgrims with notes concerning their history, Buddhist meaning, the rail fairs and routes to them as well as other travel instructions. At the height of the Society's modern pilgrimage industry during the 1930s, a wide range of such publications again appeared in *The Maha-Bodhi*. For example, Broughton (1931) wrote a long article entitled "Buddhist Pilgrimage" providing a basic north Indian itinerary, with travel descriptions (by rail, bus, cart, etc.), references to local features and the Buddhist history of each site, and was complete with quotations of the famous lines from the *Mahāparinirvāṇa-sūtra* about pilgrimage to the four main holy places associated with the historical Buddha. *The Maha-Bodhi* featured similar articles by Gunavardhana (1930), Hewavitarane (1936), and Daya Ram Sahni (1936). As part of its *Maha Bodhi Pamphlet Series*, the Society then republished S. Narain's (1937) booklet *Sarnath*, a pilgrim's guide to the site, and Dharmapala (1908, 1923a, 1923b) had published a similar series of guides to the Bodh Gayā complex, which were later reissued. The subject of the early Chinese Buddhist pilgrim accounts of India had already received coverage in *The Maha-Bodhi* at the turn of the century, see Anon (1898b), Naojiro Kitamura (1899) and Anon (1917), and it was revived again during the 1930s pilgrimage boom, see for instance Narain (1930, 1934, 1937).
33. (Anon 1931:518); see the photograph of Lama Yongden following p.70 of David-Neel (1983).
34. See, for example, the testimony of Rakra Thetong (1992:20).
35. Stoddard (1985:160-162, 175).
36. Berry (1995:287).
37. See, for example, the accounts by Khyungtrül Jigme Namkha Dorje (1897-1955) (Kvaerne 1998), Kyangtsun Sherab Namgye (c.1940s) (Ramble 1999:23-25), and the Seventh Repa Bayö (1876-1942) (Ripa Karma Bag-yod 1994).

38. The critical criteria of composition (as opposed only to actual physical production) upon which the present assignation "modern Tibetan literature" is based are discussed in Huber (1997). The category "native Tibetan" here does not include certain early works written in the Tibetan language and produced under the influence of Christian missionary activity by residents of the sub-ethnic Tibetan borderlands within colonial India, and upon which see Schubert (1935b).
39. See Huber (forthcoming) for a detailed treatment of this issue and all the sites concerned.
40. For reports of the site and its development, see: *rNam-thar* (23b-24b); *rNam-bshad* (12b, l.4-5); bTsan-po No-mon-han (1980:34b, 6-35b, 3); Waddell (1934:306-14); Tucci (1931:702); Aris (1979:112-114); Aris (1986:71-73, 77); Aris (1995:20-21, 67, n.26); cf. also Siiger (1951:9).
41. Ramble (1999:24).
42. Reported by Tucci (1940:14); and Bharati (1978:82) who witnessed "great numbers" of Tibetans there in the 1950s; cf. also Combe (1926:173). It is perhaps well to remember here that the scientific study of Indian Buddhist archaeology has also generated multiple and even spurious identifications for some sites, such as the case of Kapilavastu, site of the Buddha's royal upbringing. See for example Chakrabarti (1988:109-112) and Härtel (1991:70-80) on Piprāhwā and Tilaurakot as candidates for the site of ancient Kapilavastu.
43. dGe-'dun Chos-'phel (1938).
44. For full details see note 3 of the Notes to the Translation below.
45. On the relationship between Gendun Chöphel and Geshe Sherab Gyatso see Stoddard (1988), Khang-dkar (1992).
46. Shes-rab rGya-mtsho (1984:27)
47. Shes-rab rGya-mtsho (1984:30).
48. See Macdonald (1970:205).
49. See Barua (1969:130-131).
50. See Macdonald (1970:205, 206).
51. See Macdonald (1985:9-11).
52. See Stoddard, (1985a:185, 187, 189).

Tibetan Text and Translation of

Amdo Gendun Chöphel's

A Guide-book for Travel to the Holy Places of India

།། རྒྱ་གར་གྱི་གནས་ཆེན་ཁག་ལ་འགྲོད་པའི་ལམ་ཡིག །།

སངས་རྒྱས་མྱ་ངན་ལས་འདས་ནས་ལོ་ཉིས་སྟོང་བཞི་བརྒྱ་གྱ་དགུ་པ་
ལ་མདོ་སྨད་པ་དགེ་འདུན་ཆོས་འཕེལ་གྱིས་བྲིས་ཤིང་།

ཀ་ལི་ཀ་ཏ་ ༩ ཨེ-ཀོལ་ཛྷེ་སཀོའར།
མ་ཧཱ་བོདྷི་སོ་སཡི་ཊེ་ནས་
པར་དུ་བསྐྲུན་པའོ།།

2483 B.E.
1939 C.E.

A Guide-book for Travel to the Holy Places of India

Written by Domepa Gendun Chöphel Two Thousand Four Hundred and Eighty-Nine Years After the Buddha Passed Beyond Suffering, and

Published by
The Maha Bodhi Society,
4a College Square,
Calcutta.

2483 B.E.
1939 C.E.

[I]

[༡] ༄༅། །སངས་རྒྱས་བཅོམ་ལྡན་འདས་ལ་ཕྱག་འཚལ་ལོ།།

།མ་ཆགས་པདྨའི་སྤྱན་ལྡན་ལྷ་མིའི་གཉེན།
།སྲིད་པས་མཆོད་འོས་བསོད་ནམས་སྟོང་གི་སྐུ།
།ཤིན་ཏུ་རྣམ་དག་གསེར་གྱི་འོད་མངའ་བ།
།མཉན་ཡོད་བཞུགས་པ་དེ་ལ་ཕྱག་འཚལ་ལོ།

།གང་དུ་བདག་གི་སྟོན་པ་སྐུ་འཁྲུངས་ཤིང་།
།གང་དུ་འདྲེན་པས་བྱང་ཆུབ་མཆོག་བརྙེས་ཏེ།
།འཆི་མེད་ལམ་བསྟན་མྱ་ངན་འདས་པ་ཡི།
།རྒྱ་གར་གནས་ཆེན་རྣམས་ལ་ཕྱག་འཚལ་ལོ།

[II]

།སངས་རྒྱས་བཅོམ་ལྡན་འདས་—རང་བྱུང་གིས་བསྙེན་པར་རྫོགས་ཏེ། དབྱར་བཞི་བཅུ་ལྷག་ཙིག་འཛིག་རྟེན་དུ་འཚོ་ཞིང་བཞུགས་ནས། ཡོང་བ་ལྷ་བུའི་སྐྱེ་བོ་རྣམས་ལ་དམ་པའི་ཆོས་ཀྱི་བཀའ་མཆིད་རྒྱས་པར་མཛད་ཅིང་། གྲོད་ཀྱི་ཡུལ་ཤིང་སྣ་ལ་ཟུང་གི་ཚལ་དུ། ཕུང་པོ་ལྷག་མ་མེད་པའི་དབྱིངས་སུ་ཡོངས་སུ་མྱ་ངན་ལས་འདས་ཏེ། ལོ་ཉིས་སྟོང་བཞི་བརྒྱ་བརྒྱད་ཅུ་དང་། ཉག་མ་དགུ་དག་འདས་སོ།།

[༢] །དེས་ན་འོ་སྐོལ་ཕྱི[༡]མའི་དུས་སུ་སྐྱེས་པ། བསོད་ནམས་ཆུང་ངུའི་སྐྱེ་བོ། སངས་རྒྱས་ཀྱི་ཞལ་དངོས་སུ་མ་མཐོང་བ་དག་ནི། བདེ་བར་གཤེགས་པའི་གནས་ཆེན་བཞི་པོ་འདི་དག་ལ་མཇལ་དགོས་སོ་ཞེས—སྟོན་པ་མྱ་ངན་ལས་འདའ་ཀར་ཞལ་ཆེམས་ཀྱི་ཚུལ་དུ་གསུངས་ཏེ། ཇི་སྐད་ལུང་ཕྲན་ཚེགས་ལས།

༡) *Orig.* ཕྱེ།

[I. Invocation]

[1] Homage to the Lord Buddha!

Homage to that benefactor of gods and humans
[who] bears lotus eyes of non-attachment,
[Whose] body with a thousand virtues deserves
worship by living beings,
Possessing a radiance of purest gold,
Dwelling in Śrāvastī!

Homage to the great holy places of India,
Where my Teacher [Buddha] was born and,
Where the guide [Buddha] found supreme
enlightenment,
Taught the way to immortality, and passed beyond
suffering!

[II. The Eight Great Buddhist Pilgrimage Places]

Lord Buddha's ordination was self-arisen, and having lived on and remained in this world for more than forty rainy seasons, he gave extensive discourses on the holy Buddhist doctrine to those persons who resemble the blind. And, in the land of the Malla, at the Grove of Paired Śāla Trees (Yamakaśālavana), he passed completely beyond suffering into the realm of *nirvāṇa* without a remainder of the substratum, since which two thousand four hundred and eighty nine years have elapsed.

[2] Thus, concerning those of us who were born subsequently—beings of little merit—who have not beheld the face of the Buddha directly, the Teacher said by way of a final exhortation as he was passing beyond suffering: "One should directly encounter these four holy places of the Sugata!" And, according to what is said in the [*Vinaya*] *kṣudrakavastu*, his expansive comments include:

།དགེ་སློང་དག ང་འདས་པའི་འོག་ཏུ་གནས་བཞི་པོ་འདི་དག་ནི་རིགས་ཀྱི་བུ་དང་བུ་མོ་དད་པ་ཅན་རྣམས་ཀྱིས་ཇི་སྲིད་འཚོ་བའི་བར་དུ་འགྲོ་བར་བྱ་ཞིང་། དྲན་པར་འགྱུར་བར་བྱའོ། བཞི་གང་ཞེ་ན་-: འདིར་ནི་བཅོམ་ལྡན་འདས་འཁྲུངས་སོ། འདིར་ནི་བཅོམ་ལྡན་འདས་མངོན་པར་རྫོགས་པར་སངས་རྒྱས་སོ། འདིར་ནི་བཅོམ་ལྡན་འདས་ཀྱིས་ཆོས་ཀྱི་འཁོར་ལོ་རྣམ་པ་བཅུ་གཉིས་སུ་བསྐོར་ཏོ། འདིར་ནི་བཅོམ་ལྡན་འདས་ཡོངས་སུ་མྱ་ངན་ལས་འདས་པ་སྟེ། དགེ་སློང་དག་ང་འདས་པའི་འོག་ཏུ་འདིར་མཆོད་རྟེན་བསྐོར་བ་དང་། མཆོད་རྟེན་ལ་ཕྱག་འཚལ་བ་དག་འོང་གི དེ་དག་ལ་འདི་སྐད་ཅེས་བརྗོད་པར་བྱ་སྟེ། ཞེས་པ་ནས་ང་ལ་དད་པས་དུས་བྱས་པ་དེ་ཐམས་ཅད་ཀྱང་བདེ་འགྲོ་མཐོ་རིས་ཀྱི་འཇིག་རྟེན་དུ་འགྲོའོ། སོགས་རྒྱས་པར་གསུངས་སོ།

།དེ་བཞིན་དུ་མདོ་གཞན་ལས་ཀྱང་-:ང་མྱ་ངན་ལས་འདས་པའི་རྗེས་སུ། དགེ་སློང་གསར་བུ་འགའ་ཞིག་འོང་ནས། ཁྱེད་ཀྱི་ [༡] སྟོན་པ་ཇི་འདྲ་ཞེས་འདྲི་ན། དེ་དག་ལ་གནས་བཞི་པོ་འདི་དག་བསྟན་པར་བྱ་སྟེ་སོགས་གསུངས་ལ།

།རྟོག་གེ་འབར་བར་མདོ་དྲངས་པ་ལས་ཀྱང་-:གནས་བཞི་པོ་འདི་དག་བསྐོར་བས་མཚམས་མེད་པའི་སྡིག་པ་ཡང་འབྱུང་བར་གསུངས་སོ།

།དེ་ལྟར་ན། རྡོ་རྗེ་གདན་ནི་བདག་ཅག་གི་སྟོན་པ་མངོན་པར་སངས་རྒྱས་པའི་གནས་ཡིན་ལ། ལུམྦི་ནི་སྐུ་འཁྲུངས་པ། ཝཱ་ར་ཎ་སི་ཆོས་འཁོར་བསྐོར་བ། ཛཾ་མཆོག་གྲོང་མྱ་ངན་ལས་འདས་པའི་གནས་ཏེ། མདོ་ལས་གསུངས་པའི་སངས་རྒྱས་ཀྱི་གནས་ཆེན་བཞི་པོ་ནི་དེ་དག་ཡིན་ལ། དེའི་སྟེང་དུ། ནཱ་ལནྡཱ་སྐུ་ཚེ་བྱིན་གྱིས་རློབས་པའི་གནས། མཉན་ཡོད་བདུད་བཏུལ་བའི་གནས། ཤང་ཁ་ས་ལྷ་ལས་བབས་པའི་གནས། རྒྱལ་པོའི་ཁབ་དབྱེན་བསྙམ་པའི་གནས་ཏེ། བརྒྱད་པོ་དེ་ནི་གནས་ཆེན་བརྒྱད་ཅེས་གྲགས་པ་དག་ཡིན་ལ། བདེ་གཤེགས་མཆོད་རྟེན་བརྒྱད་དུ་གྲགས་པ་དག་ཀྱང་། སྔར་གནས་ཆེན་འདི་དག་ན་བཞུགས་པ་ཡིན་ནོ།

> "O Monks, after my passing there are these four places which sons and daughters of good family who possess faith should visit and recollect for as long as they live. What are the four? [The places where, as pilgrims, they will say:] 'Here the Lord took birth. Here the Lord attained complete buddhahood. Here the Lord turned the wheel of Buddhist doctrine with twelve aspects. Here the Lord passed completely beyond suffering.' O monks, this should be told to those who come to these places after my passing, and who sincerely circumambulate and perform prostrations to my funerary monuments (*stūpa*) at these places." Further, "All those who [do so, and] die with faith in me, will proceed to a heavenly realm of existence."[1]

Similarly, in other *sūtra*-s as well he stated such thing as, "When some novice monks appear after my passing beyond suffering, **[3]** if they ask: 'What was your Teacher like?', they should be shown these four places."

Also, according to a *sūtra* quoted in the *Tarkajvālā*[2] he stated, "By circumambulating these four places even the five transgressions incurring immediate retribution will be cleansed."

Thus, Vajrāsana is the place of our Teacher's manifest buddhahood, he was born at Lumbinī, he turned the wheel of Buddhist doctrine in Vārāṇasī (i.e. Sārnāth), and Kuśinagarī is the place where he passed beyond suffering. Those are the four holy places of the Buddha which he spoke of in the *sūtra*-s and, in addition to them, Nālandā is the place where he supernaturally controlled his life span,[3] Śrāvastī is the place where he conquered evil, Sāṃkāśya is the place he descended from among the gods, and Rājagṛha is the place where he reconciled a schism. Those eight are famous as the "Eight Holy Places", and they are also famous for the eight funerary monuments of the Tathāgata which were present at these holy places in the past.

[III.]

གནས་ཆེན་བཞི་པོ་འདིའི་ནོད་ཐུབ་རེ་ཧྥར་མའི་ཡུལ་དང་། རྒྱ་གར་ཤར་ན་ཡང་ཡོད་ཅིང་། དེ་མཚུངས་རྒྱ་གར་ནུབ་དང་། ཞམ་ཡུལ་སོགས་སུ་ཡང་ཡོད་མོད་ཀྱི། རྩ་བའི་གནས་ཆེན་རྣམས་ནི་རྒྱ་གར་དབུས་ཀྱི་འདི་དག་འཁྲུལ་མེད་དེ་ཡིན་པ་ནི། དཔེར་ན་རྡོ་རྗེ་གདན་ལྷ་བུ་གཅིག་ལ་མཚོན་ན་ཡང་། ལོ་ [༤] སྟོང་གི་སྔར་ཐོན་པའི་རྒྱལ་བཙུན་པ་ཕྭ་ཧེན་དང་། ཐང་ཟན་ཙང་དང་། ཨི་ཙང་རྣམས་ཀྱི་ལམ་ཡིག་དང་། བོད་ཀྱི་ལོ་ཙཱ་[༢] བ་ཆག་ཆོས་རྗེ་དཔལ་གྱི་ལམ་ཡིག་རྒྱས་པ། བཅོམ་ལྡན་རིག་རལ་གྱི་རྡོ་རྗེ་གདན་རྒྱས་བཤད་རྣམས་དང་། དེར་མ་ཟད་སྔར་ཐང་[༣] དགོན་ན་རྡོ་ནག་ལས་གྲུབ་པའི་རྡོ་རྗེ་གདན་གྱི་གནས་བཀོད་རྒྱ་གར་ནས་གདན་དྲངས་པ་ཞིག་དང་། མཆིམས་ནམ་མཁའ་གྲགས་པའི་ཞལ་བཀོད་བཞིན་ཙན་དན་ལས་བྱས་པའི་རྡོ་རྗེ་གདན་གྱི་བཀོད་པ་རྒྱ་ནག་ནས་གདན་དྲངས་པ་གཅིག་བཅས་བཞུགས་པ། དེ་ཐམས་ཅད་བསྡུར་ཚེ། ཕན་ཚུན་གཅིག་ལ་གཅིག་ངོ་འཕྲོད་དེ། མི་གཅིག་གིས་བྱས་པ་དང་འདྲ་བར་ཡོད་པས་དོགས་པ་ཙམ་ཡང་ག་ལ་འོས།

དེས་ན་འགའ་ཞིག་ནི་ཡུལ་འདིར་དངོས་སུ་ཐོན་ཏེ། ཡུན་རིང་བཞུགས་པའི་སྔོན་གྱི་ལོ་ཙཱ་[༤] བ་ཚད་ཐུབ་དེ་དག་གི་གསུང་ལ་རྒྱུས་ཚུད་ཟད་ཀྱང་མེད་པར། ཨ་ཙ་རའི་ངག་སྒྲོས་བསགས་པ་དང་། གྲུབ་ཐོབ་འགའ་རེ་དག་སྣང་ལ་དེར་ཐོན་ཏེ། ཡ་མཚན་མང་དུ་གཟི་ཊ་པར་གསུངས་པའི་གཏམ་རེ་གཉིས་ལ་ཁྲུངས་སུ་བྱས་ཏེ་གནས་ཆེན་འདི་རྣམས་དངོས་མ་ཡིན་མིན་གྱི་དོགས་པ་བསྐྱེད་པ་ནི་ཤིན་ཏུ་ཡང་མ་ལེགས་ཏེ། དག་པའི་སྣང་བ་ནི་ལས་དག་ན་མཐོང་བ་ཡིན་པས། སྨོན་པར་བྱ་བ་ཙམ་དུ་འོས་མོད། རང་ཅག་ཕལ་པའི་མཐོང་སྣང་ལ་ཞུ་དག་གཏོང་བའི་ཁྲུངས་སུ་ག་ལ་རུང་། སྤྲུལ་པའི་ལུས་ཐོབ་ན། ཁབ་ཀྱི་མིག་ཏུ་ཡང་སངས་རྒྱས་ཀྱི་ཞིང་ཁམས་བགྲོད་ནུས་པས།

༢) *Orig.* ཙ།
༣) *Orig.* ཐར།
༤) *Orig.* རྩ།

[III. Representations and Reality]

Although there are some substitutes for these [first aforementioned] four holy places in the country of Burma and in eastern India, and indeed even others like them in western India and in the country of Siam, the original holy places are indisputably these central Indian ones.[4] As for that being so, for example, even if we take an instance like Vajrāsana: **[4]** There are travel accounts of it by the Chinese monks Fa-hsien (travelled 399-414), Hsüan-tsang (in India 629-645), and I-ching (travelled 671-695) who went there prior to a thousand years ago; and there is the extensive travel account by the Tibetan translator Chag Chöjepal (1197-1264) and the extensive explanation of Vajrāsana by Chomden Rigrel (c.1250-1311);[5] and still further, at Narthang monastery there is a model of Vajrāsana made out of black stone which had been brought from India, as well as a model of Vajrāsana fashioned from sandalwood which had been brought from China on account of the orders of Chim Namkha Dagpa (1210-1285).[6] When we put all of them together, compare them one to the other and recognize them [as representing exactly the same site], since they are like the work of one person how could it be worthwhile at all to have doubts?

Therefore, concerning some who came in person to this country and had not even the slightest familiarity with the statements of those reliable translators of the past who had made prolonged stays there, they collected the utterances of the spiritual masters and a few Tantric adepts went there in pure visions. They were the source for several accounts which relate many remarkable sights, and it is highly inappropriate to generate doubts about whether or not those holy places [they envisioned] were the real ones. Visions which are pure are perceived when one's *karma* is pure, therefore one ought only to desire them! How could it be appropriate for our mundane perceptions to be the source for making corrections to visions? If one obtains an emanation-body one is capable of travelling to a Buddha realm, even through the eye of a needle,

དེ་འདྲ་བ་ཞི་རང་ཅག་གདོས་བཅས་ཤ་ [༥] ཁྲག་གི་ཕུང་པོ་ཉིན་མཚན་[༥] འབྲལ་མེད་དུ་འཁྱེར་བཞིན་པ་རྣམས་ཀྱིས། (བཙལ་བའི་འོས་ཀྱང་མ་ཡིན་ལ། སྨོད་པའི་འོས་ཀྱང་མ་ཡིན་ནོ།།)

[IV]

།དེ་ལ་རྡོ་རྗེ་གདན་ནི་གནས་འདི་ཀུན་གྱི་གཙོ་བོ་ཡིན་པས་ཅུང་ཙམ་ཞིབ་པར་བཤད་ན། དེ་ཡང་གན་རྡྷོ་ལ་འདི་ཐོག་མར་བྲམ་ཟེ་མོ་ཛ་སའི་བུ་ཐ་ཆུང་གིས་བཞེངས་ཀྱང་ཟེར། ཆོས་རྒྱལ་མྱ་ངན་མེད་ཀྱིས་ཡིན་ཡང་ཟེར། གང་ལྟར་ཀྱང་བར་སྐབས་ཞིག་ན་ཤིན་ཏུ་ཉམས་ཆགས་སུ་གྱུར་བ་ལས། མ་ག་དྷའི་ཁྲིམ་བདག་འཆི་མེད་བྱ་བ་ཞིག་གིས་ཞིག་གསོས་བགྱིས་ཏེ་ད་བར་ལོ་སྟོང་ཕྲག་ལྷག་ཙམ་སོང་། དེ་ནས་སླར་ཡང་ཉམས་པ་ན། ཧྥར་མའི་ཡུལ་གྱི་ནང་པ་རྣམས་ནས་ཞིག་གསོས་བགྱིས་ཏེ་ད་བར་ལོ་དྲུག་བརྒྱ་ལྷག་སོང་། དེ་ནས་སླར་ཡང་རྒྱ་གར་གཞུང་ནས་སྐྱོར་ཉིས་འབུམ་ལྷག་གི་འགྲོ་སོང་བཏང་སྟེ། ས་བསལ་ཅིང་ཞིག་རལ་བཅོས་ཏེ་ད་ལྟ་ལོ་བཞི་བཅུ་ལྷག་སོང་།།

།དབུས་ཀྱི་གན་རྡྷོ་ལའི་རྩེའི་མཆོད་རྟེན་ཆུང་ངུ་དེ་ཀླུ་སྒྲུབ་ཀྱིས་བཞེངས་ཤིང་ནང་དུ་སྟོན་པའི་རིང་བསྲེལ་བྲེ་གང་བཞུགས། ལྷ་ཁང་སྟེང་འོག་གཉིས་ཡོད་པའི་སྟེང་མ་དེའི་ནང་དུ་རང་རེའི་ལྷ་སའི་ཇོ་བོ་སྟོན་བཞུགས་པར་གྲགས། བསྐོར་ལམ་གྱི་རྡོའི་ད྄[༦] མིག་འདི་དག་ཀྱང་ཀླུ་སྒྲུབ་ཀྱིས་བཞེངས། ཀ་[༧] བ་དེ་དག་གི་སྟེང་ན་མགོན་པོའི་ཞལ་བརྒྱད་དང་སྒྲོལ་མའི་ཞལ་བརྒྱད་ཡོད་པ་མི་གཅིག་གིས་དེ་ཐམས་ཅད་མཐོང་ན་དངོས་གྲུབ་ སྣ་རེ་ཐོབ་ཟེར། དེ་དག་ནི་པད་ཀོར་གྱི་དཀྱིལ་ [༦] ན་མིའི་གདོང་ལྷ་བུ་ཡོད་པ་དེ་རྣམས་ཡིན།

---

༥) *Orig.* སཚན།

༦) *Orig.* ད྄།

༧) *Orig.* ཀྲ།

but because we are carrying inseparably, day and night, the corporeal aggregates of flesh **[5]** and blood, we are not even worthy to search after the likes of that, let alone disparage it!

[IV. Bodh Gayā]

Because Vajrāsana is foremost among all these places, I will explain precisely a little about it. So, although it is said that initially this [Mahābodhi] *caitya*-temple[7] was erected by the youngest son of the brahmin woman Jaḥsā, it is also said to have been done by the Buddhist monarch Aśoka (c.273-236 B.C.E.).[8] Be that as it may, after a time it became completely derelict, and thus a householder from Magadha named Amara restored it, and that was just over a thousand years ago. After that, when it had deteriorated once more, it was restored by Buddhists from the land of Burma and that was more than six hundred years ago.[9] After that, the Indian government once again spent over 200,000 *rupees* clearing the site and renovating the ruins, and that was over forty years ago.[10]

The small funerary monument at the apex of the central *caitya*-temple was erected by Nāgārjuna (c. 2nd cent. A.D.),[11] and within it there are contained one measure of the Teacher's relics.[12] There exist two chapels, upper and lower, of which it is the upper one that is famous [in Tibet] since our own [statue] of the Lord in the Lhasa [Jokhang temple] previously resided inside it.[13] The stone railings of the circumambulation path were also erected by Nāgārjuna.[14] On top of the columns [supporting the railings] there are eight faces of Mahākāla and eight faces of Tārā.[15] If one person sees all of them it is said they will obtain a type of paranormal power. Concerning them, they resemble human faces in **[6]** the centre of lotus surrounds.

དེ་ལ་སྟོན་པ་སངས་རྒྱས་ནས་བདུན་ཕྲག་དང་པོ་ལ་བྱང་ཆུབ་ཤིང་ལ་སྤྱན་མིག་འཛུམ་པར་བཞུགས་པའི་སྐུ་བརྙན་ནི་བྱང་ཆུབ་ཤིང་གི་ཐད་ཀྱི་མཆོད་རྟེན་ངོས་ན་བཞུགས་པ་དེ་ཡིན་ལ། བདུན་གཉིས་པར་དང་པོ་བཞེངས་པའི་ཤུལ་དུ་ཞབས་རྗེས་ཆ་གཅིག དེ་ནས་གོམ་པ་དོར་པའི་ཤུལ་ཞབས་གཡས་གཡོན་ཡ་སྦྱིལ་པ་ལྔ་། སླར་ཡང་ཡུད་ཙམ་བཞེངས་སར་ཞབས་ཆ་གཅིག་བཅས་རྡོ་བདུན་གྱི་སྟེང་དུ་ཡོད་པ་ལས་དེང་སང་ཡ་གཉིས་དང་ཆ་གཅིག་སྟེ་གསུམ་ཙམ་ཡོད། དེ་ནས་ཞབས་འཆག་པའི་ཤུལ་བསྐོར་ལམ་བྱང་གི་སྟེགས་རིང་པོའི་སྟེང་ན་པདྨའི་ཕྲེང་བ་བཅུ་གཉིས་ཡོད།

།བྱང་ངོས་དྲ་[༡] མིག་གི་ཕྱི་རོལ་དུ་མཆོད་རྟེན་ཆུང་ངུ་བུ་ག་ཡོད་པ་དེ་དག་གི་ནང་ན་དགྲ་བཅོམ་མང་པོའི་གདུང་བཞུགས་ཤིང་སྲ་སེན་སོགས་དེར་འཕང་ན་ངན་སོང་གི་སྐྱེ་སྒོ་ཁེགས་པར་བཤད།

།མཆོད་རྟེན་གྱི་ཤར་ཕྱོགས་རྭ་བའི་འདབས་ན་དབུས་མ་དང་དབྱིབས་འདྲ་བའི་མཆོད་རྟེན་ཆེན་པོ་ཞིག་ཡོད་པ་དེ་སྟོན་པ་དང་པོར་བྱོན་སྐབས་དེར་བཞུགས་ཏེ་ཞལ་ནས་འོད་ཟེར་སྤྲོས་ནས་བྱང་ཆུབ་ཤིང་དངོས་མ་མིན་པ་གཞན་རྣམས་སྲིགས་པའི་གནས་ཡིན། དེ་ལ་འོད་ཟེར་འཕྲོ་བའི་གན་རྫོ་ལ་[༢] ཟེར། དེ་ལྟར་ཤིང་ཚིག་པ་རྣམས་ཀྱི་སོལ་བ་སྤུངས་པའི་སར་ཨ་ཀར་བོ་ཏྲི་བྱ་བའི་བྱང་ཆུབ་ཤིང་ཞིག་སྐྱེས་པ་ [༥] ད་ལྟ་བྱང་ངོས་སྐོར་ལམ་གྱི་ཕྱི་ན་ཡོད་པ་དེ་ཡིན། ཤིང་དེའི་རྩར་ར་ས་ཀུ་ལའི་གྲོན་པ་ཡོད། དེའི་ཆུ་སྟོན་པས་རྫུ་འཕྲུལ་གྱིས་དངུལ་ཆུར་བྱིན་གྱིས་རློབས་འབྱུང་ན་ཡོ་ནད་དྲག་ཟེར། གྲོན་པ་མ་བྲུས་ཀྱང་ཁ་བྲེར་གསལ་བར་ཡོད། འོན་ཀྱང་ལོ་ཤས་འདིའི་འོག་ཏུ་འདག་ཞལ་བྱས་ཟེར་འདུག

༡) *Orig.* དྲ།

༢) *Orig.* ལེ། The exchange of terminal ལེ་ for ལ་ in this word is recurrent in the account of ཆག་ལོ་ཙཱ་བ་ which our author resorted to (e.g. see Roerich 1959: 13-14).

As for the statue there of the Teacher, when he sat with his eyes closed under the Bodhi Tree for the first week after his enlightenment, it is situated on the face of the funerary monument which is directly at the Bodhi Tree. And, there are a set of foot prints as the trace of his initial arising in the second week, then a total of five single left and right foot prints as traces of his striding forth. Together with a set of foot prints on the ground where he arose for just one moment afterwards, there were seven [foot prints] on stone, out of which nowadays there are two single ones and a set, just three existing.[16] Tracing his footsteps from there is a garland of twelve lotus flowers on top of a long embankment to the north of the circumambulation path.[17]

On the outside of the railings, facing north, there are small funerary monuments with niches. Within them reside the relics of many Arhats, and if one throws such things as hair[18] and fingernails into them it is said that the doors to rebirth in the unfortunate realms of existence will be closed.

At the side of the perimeter fence, east of the [above small] funerary monuments, there is a large funerary monument which resembles the [*caitya*-temple] shape of the central one. When the Teacher first came here he dwelt there, and it is the place where he incinerated all the other trees which were not genuine Bodhi Trees when he emitted rays of light from his mouth. Thus it is called the Light Radiation Caitya-temple.[19] Accordingly, at the spot where the charcoal of the burnt trees was heaped up, a Bodhi Tree which is named the Agaru Bodhi sprouted.[20] **[7]** Nowadays, it is that one which exists outside of the circumambulation path, facing north.[21] At the base of that tree is the well of Rasakula. Its waters were magically transformed into quicksilver (*rasa*) by the Teacher's magical powers. It is said that when drunk it is good for stomach ailments. Although the well has not been dug its edges are evident. Nevertheless, several years [ago] mud was plastered beneath it and seems to be holding.

མཆོད་རྟེན་དབུས་མའི་ལྷོ་ངོར་ས་སྟེགས་ཤིན་ཏུ་ཡངས་པ་ཞིག་ཡོད་པ་དེར་སྟོན་པའི་བཞུགས་གདན་གྱི་རྗེ་རྣམས་པོར། དེར་སྟོན་མཆོད་རྟེན་དབུས་ཀྱི་འདི་དང་འདྲ་བའི་ཆེན་པོ་ཞིག་ཡོད་པ་ཡིན།

།ནྭ་བའི་ཤར་གྱི་དུར་[༡༠] ཁྲོད་ནང་གི་དཀྱིལ་འཁོར་དེ་སློབ་དཔོན་སངས་རྒྱས་ཡེ་ཤེས་ཀྱིས་རྡོ་ལ་བཞེངས་པའི་དུས་འཁོར་བློས་བསླང་རྡོ་རྗེ་གདན་དུ་ཡོད་ཅེས་རང་རེའི་ལོ་རྒྱུས་འགའ་ལས་འབྱུང་བ་དེ་ཡིན་ནམ་སྙམ།

།འདི་ཙམ་ཞིག་ཆག་ཡོད་དང་བཅོམ་ལྡན་རིག་རལ་སོགས་ཀྱི་གསུང་དང་ཡང་འཕགས་པར་འགྱུར་བས་ཡིད་ཆེས་པའི་གནས་ཡིན་ལ་གཞན་མང་དུ་བཤད་པར་དཀའ།

།དེ་[༡༡] ཡང་ཆག་ཆོས་དཔལ་སོགས་བྱོན་སྐབས་གཙུག་ལག་ཁང་འདི་དར་རྒྱས་ཀྱི་སྐབས་ཡིན་ལ། དགེ་སློང་སུམ་བརྒྱ་ཙམ་རེ་རྒྱུན་དུ་དཀོན་གཉེར་གྱི་ཚུལ་ཏུ་བཞུགས་ཅེས་གསུངས།

[༥] །དེ་ནས་དུས་ཀྱི་རྒྱུད་པས་གནས་གཞི་རྟེན་དང་བཅས་པ་མུ་སྟེགས་ཀྱི་ཧོ་ཀི་དག་གི་ལག་པར་ཤོར། མཆོད་རྟེན་གྱི་གསེབ་ཏུ་ཕྱི་རོལ་པའི་ལྷ་ཁང་བརྩིགས། གཙུག་ལག་ཁང་དུ་དབང་ཕྱུག་གི་རྟེན་འཛུགས་པ་དང་ཁྲག་མཆོད་བྱེད་པ་སོགས་མི་འཚམ་པ་དུ་མ་བྱས་པར་དགེ་བསྙེན་[༡༢] དྷརྨ་པཱ་ལ་ནས་ཐུགས་ཀྱིས་མ་བཟོད་པར། སྔར་ཡང་ནང་པ་རྣམས་ཀྱི་རང་བདག་ཏུ་ཐོབ་པའི་ཆེད་དུ་འབད་པ་ཆེན་པོས་ཁྲིམས་གཏུགས་སོགས་བྱེད་མུས་ལ་སྐུ་གཤེགས།

།ད་དུང་ཡང་སྔར་རྩོལ་དེ་ཀ་བྱེད་དང་བྱེད་མུས་ལགས་ཀྱང་ད་བར་རེ་འབྲས་གཙང་སྨིན་ཅི་ཡང་མ་བྱུང་བས། རང་རེ་རྒྱལ་ཁབ་ཀུན་གྱི་སངས་རྒྱས་པ་རྣམས་ལས་དང་འདུན་པ་གཅིག་དྲིལ་གྱི་སྒོ་ནས། རང་ཅག་རྣམས་ཀྱི་ཁོང་པའི་སྙིང་དང་འདྲ་བའི་བྱིན་རླབས་ཀྱི་གནས་ཆེན་ཁྱད་པར་ཅན་འདི་ཉིད་འོས་པའི་བདག་པོ་སངས་རྒྱས་པ་རྣམས་ཀྱི་རང་ལག་ཏུ་ཐོབ་པ་ཞིག་ལ་ཅིས་ཀྱང་འབད་དགོས།

---

༡༠) *Orig.* དུད།
༡༡) *Orig.* དེང་།
༡༢) *Orig.* བཀྙེན

On the south side of the central funerary monument there is a very broad area of raised ground. On that spot the Teacher threw down [*kuśa*] grass as a seating mat. At that place, in the past, there existed at large funerary monument which was similar to the central one.

There is a *maṇḍala* which is inside the charnel ground to the east of the perimeter fence. According to statements in some of our [Tibetan] histories, "That meditative outline *maṇḍala* of *Kālacakra* which was raised in stone by the meditation master Buddhajñāna (8th cent.) exists at Vajrāsana." It is thought it could be that.

Because this agrees well also with the statements of Chag Lotsawa, Chomden Rigrel, and so on, it is a credible holy site, although it is difficult to say so about many others.

Specifically: When the likes of Chag Chöjepal arrived there, this monastic centre was in a period of development, and he reported "About three hundred fully ordained monks residing [there], in the manner of sacristans, at all times."[22]

[8] Due to the decline in the period after that, the site, together with its sacred representations, passed into the hands of heretic (i.e. Śaiva) yogins. A non-Buddhist temple was built among the funerary monuments. Many disagreeable things were done in the monastic centre, including setting up an image of Īśvara and performing blood sacrifices, and as the Buddhist layman Dharmapāla (1864-1933) found this unbearable he strove greatly for the purpose of placing it under the control of Buddhists once again, thus engaging in such things as legal action, in the course of which he passed away.

Yet, even though the very same endeavour as before is being made and continues to be made, up until now the pure fruits of [Dharmapāla's] hopes have not by any means begun to ripen. Therefore, by way of our combined deeds and intentions, we Buddhists of all nations should strive by all means to get this same superior holy place [of Bodh Gayā] which is empowered just like the hearts that are inside of us, [back] into the hands of its lawful Buddhists owners!

[V]

༡ རྡོ་རྗེ་གདན་གྱི་ལམ་ཟུར་བྱེ་མ་ལ་རྒྱུ་བའི་ཆུ་བོ་དེ་ནེརཉྫ་ན་སྟེ་ཆུ་འགྲམ་དེར་སྔོན་པས་ལོ་དྲུག་དཀའ་བ་སྤྱད་ཅིང་། སྤྱིར་གཱ་ཡའི་ཕྱོགས་འདིར་སངས་རྒྱས་ལོ་བདུན་ཙམ་བཞུགས། གཱ་ཡའི་གྲོང་ཁྱེར་གྱི་བྱང་ངོས་ན་མཐོང་བའི་རི་དེ་རྣམས་གཱ་ཡ་ཤིརྵ་སྟེ་གཱ་ཡ་མགོ་རི་བྱ་བ་དེ་ཡིན། རྡོ་རྗེ་གདན་ནས་ཤར་ལྷོ་ཕྱོགས་སུ་མེ་ལེ་བདུན་ཙམ་སོང་ན་དུཀྟཱཤྲཱི་བྱ་བ་དང་ལྷའི་དུར་ཁྲོད་བསིལ་བ་ཚལ་དེ་ཡོད། [༡]

[VI]

༢ ཤེ་ལེ་གུ་རི་ནས་རྡོ་རྗེ་གདན་དུ་འོངས་པའི་ལམ་དུ་གཏྣ་བཏལ་མ་ཐག་པ་ཊ་ཎ་ལ་སླེབས། དེ་ནི་ཆོས་རྒྱལ་ (ཨཤོཀ་) མྱ་ངན་མེད་ཅེས་བྱ་བ་འཛམ་བུ་གླིང་དུ་མཆོད་རྟེན་བྱེ་བ་བཞེངས་མཁན་དེའི་རྒྱལ་ས་ཡིན། སྔོན་གྲོང་ཁྱེར་པ་ཊ་ལི་པུ་ཏྲ་ཞེས་ཟེར་ཞིང་བོད་སྐད་དུ་སྐྱ་ནར་བུའི་གྲོང་ཁྱེར་བྱ་བ་དེ་ཡིན། རྒྱལ་པོ་མྱ་ངན་མེད་ཀྱི་ཕོ་བྲང་གི་ཤུལ་དང་གཞན་ཡང་གྲོང་ཁྱེར་གྱི་མུ་ཟེམ་ཁང་ (MUSEUM) གི་ནང་དུ་སྔོན་གྱི་སྐུ་བརྙན་ངོ་མཚར་ཅན་མང་པོ་དང་། མྱ་ངན་མེད་ཀྱི་བཙུན་མོའི་འདྲ་བརྙན་ཡིན་ནམ་ཟེར་བའི་རྡོ་སྐུ་ཤེལ་ལྟར་འཚེར་བ་ཞིག་ཀྱང་ཡོད།

[VII]

༣ པ་ཊ་ཎ་ནས་ར་ཛེ་གི་རི་ལ་འགྲོ་བའི་ལམ་དུ་བི་ཧར་ཤ་རིབ་—(BIHAR-SHARIF) ཟེར་བའི་གྲུ་ཟན་ལ་སླེབས་ཅིང་དེ་ནས་ནུབ་ཏུ་བལྟས་ན་བྲག་རི་ལེབ་མོ་ཞིག་མཐོང་བ་དེ་ཨོཏནྟཔུརིའི་གཙུག་ལག་ཁང་གི་ཤུལ་ཡིན་ཟེར། སྔོན་གཙུག་ལག་ཁང་དེ་རྒྱ་གར་ན་གྲགས་པ་ཞིག་ཡིན་ཅིང་རང་རེའི་བོད་ཀྱི་བསམ་ཡས་ཀྱང་དེ་ལ་དཔེ་བྱས་ཏེ་བཞེངས་པ་ཡིན།

[V. Gayā]

1. The river which meanders along the sandy road-sides of Vajrāsana is the Nairañjanā, and the Teacher performed austerities for six year on that river bank [i.e. at Uruvilvā]. In all, the Buddha stayed for about seven years on this side of Gayā. Those hills which are visible to the north of the town of Gayā are the Gayāśīrṣa, and they are the ones [we Tibetans call] Gāyagori. If one proceeds almost seven miles in a south-easterly direction from Vajrāsana, there is the charnel ground of Cool Grove (Śītavana) which is presently known as Durgāśrī.[23] **[9]**

[VI. Patna]

2. On the route which goes to Vajrāsana from Silīguri, one arrives in Patna immediately after crossing the Gangā. That place was the imperial capital of the Buddhist monarch known as Aśoka, Nyanenmé [in Tibetan], who was the builder of ten million funerary monuments throughout the Southern Continent (Jambudvīpa).[24] The ancient city was called Pāṭaliputra, and in Tibetan it is known as the city of Kyanarbu. In the ruins of king Aśoka's palace, and furthermore in the city MUSEUM, there are many amazing ancient statues, and a likeness of Aśoka's queen, or at least there is a stone image shining like crystal which is said to be it.

[VII. Odantapurī]

3. On the route which goes to Rājgir from Patna one arrives at the [railway] station[25] which is named [and pronounced] "Bi-har-sha-rib" BIHAR-SHARIF, and if one looks to the west from there one sees a flat rock hill. That is said to be the ruins of the monastic centre of Odantapurī. In the past, that monastic centre was a famous one in India, and we in Tibet modeled and built the Samye [monastery] after it as well.

ས་འདི་ཡིན་ཟེར་བ་ཙམ་ལས་གནས་ཀྱི་ཞུལ་ལ་སོ་ཏ་པ་ནི་མི་སྣང་། རི་འདི་ནི་ནཱ་རོ་པའི་བཞུགས་གནས་ཕུ་ལ་ཧ་རི་བྱ་བ་དེ་ཡིན་པར་ཐེ་ཚོམ་མི་འདུག་སྙེ། ཆག་ལོའི་རྣམ་ཐར་དུ་ན་ལནྡྲའི་བྱང་ངོས་ཚ་འབོག་གཅིག་གི་ས་ན་རི་དེ་ཡོད་གསུངས་ཞིང་། ན་ལནྡྲའི་བྱང་ན་རི་འདི་གཅིག་བུ་མ་གཏོགས་ཡེ་མེད་ལ། རིའི་དབྱིབས་ཀྱང་ [༡༠] བོད་ཀྱི་ཕྱོགས་སུ་མགོ་གུག་པ་ལྟར་ཡོད་པས་མི་ལའི་རྣམ་ཐར་དང་ཡང་འགྲིག །

[VIII]

༤ དེ་ནས་ན་ལནྡྲ་ལའི་གྲུ་ཟན་ལ་སླེབས་ཀང་ཐང་ལ་ཚུང་ཟད་སོང་ན་སྟོན་གྱི་དགོན་ཞུལ་རྒྱ་ཆེན་པོ་ཡོད། ན་ལནྡྲ་ནི་སྟོན་རྒྱ་གར་གྱི་ཆོས་སྡེ་ཐམས་ཅད་ཀྱི་གཙོ་བོ་ཡིན་ཞིང་རྒྱ་ནག་གི་བཙུན་པ་ཐང་ཟན་ཙང་ཕེབས་པའི་དུས་དགེ་སློང་ཁྲི་ཕྲག་ཙམ་བཞུགས་ཞེས་ཟེར། ཨཏི་ཤ། ཞི་བ་འཚོ། སློབ་དཔོན་ཆེན་པོ། ཟླ་བ་གྲགས་པ་ལ་སོགས་པའི་སྟོན་གྱི་པཎྜིཏ་ཆེན་པོ་དེ་ཐམས་ཅད་ཀྱང་དགོན་པ་འདི་ནས་ཕེབས་པ་ཞ་སྟག་ཡིན། བོད་དང་རྒྱ་ནག་ཏུ་དམ་པའི་ཆོས་དར་བ་ཡང་དང་པོ་དགོན་པ་འདི་ནས་བྱུང་བ་ཡིན།

[IX]

༥ ན་ལནྡྲ་ནས་ར་ཛ་གི་རི་ལ་སླེབས། དེ་ནི་རྒྱལ་པོའི་ཁབ་ཡིན་ཞིང་དེར་རིས་བསྐོར་བའི་དབུས་ཀྱི་ཐང་དེ་ཐམས་ཅད་སྟོན་གྲོང་ཁྱེར་ཆགས་པའི་ཞུལ་ཡིན། ཕྲར་མའི་ཧྲམ་སྣུ་ལ་དང་ཉེ་བ་ན་སྟོན་གྱི་རྡོ་མཁར་ཆེན་པོ་ཞིག་ཡོད་པ་དེ་རྒྱལ་པོའི་ཁབ་གསར་པ་བྱ་བ་རྒྱལ་པོ་(ཨཛྷ་ཏ་ཤ་ཏྲུ་) མ་སྐྱེས་དགྲའི་ཕོ་བྲང་གི་ཞུལ་ཡིན། ཆུ་ཚན་གྱི་གནས་དེ་ཆུ་དྲོན་གྱི་ཀུན་དགའ་ར་བའི་ཞུལ་དང་།

Other than it just being said to be this spot, such things as the ruins of the site are not in evidence.[26] Concerning this hill, it is without a doubt that place of residence of Nāropa (956-1040) known as Pulahari. In the biography of Chag Lotsawa it states that hill is at a spot which is a half-day's walk to the north of Nālandā,[27] and north of Nālandā, except for this single hill there are none at all. And, the form of the hill also **[10]** has an appearance as though its summit is bent in the direction of Tibet, thus it corresponds also with the [description in] Mila[repa's] (1040-1123) biography.[28]

[VIII. Nālandā]

4. From there, one arrives at the [railway] station which is at Nālandā. If one proceeds a little way on foot, there are very extensive ruins of the ancient monastery. As for Nālandā, in the past it was foremost of all the Buddhist religious communities of India, and at the time of the journey of the Chinese monk Hsüan-tsang it was said to have as many as ten thousand fully-ordained monks in residence.[29] All the great scholars of the past as well, including Āryadeva, Śāntarakṣita (8th cent.), Padmasambhava and Candrakīrti (c.600-660), came exclusively from this monastery. The diffusion of the holy Buddhist doctrine to Tibet and China also originated from this monastery first.

[IX. Rājagṛha]

5. From Nālandā one arrives at Rājgir. That place is Rājagṛha, and here the whole central plain which is encircled by hills contains the remains of the ancient city foundations (see figure 3). Close to the Burmese pilgrims rest-house (*dharmaśālā*) there is a large, ancient stone fort. That is known as New Rājagṛha;[30] and is the ruin of king Ajātaśatru's palace. The site of the hot springs there is the remains of the Warm Water Pleasure Garden (Tapodārāma),

ཆུ་ཚན་ཡོད་སའི་རི་དེ་རྒྱལ་པོའི་ཁབ་ཀྱི་རི་ལྔའི་ནང་གི་བཻ་པུ་ལ་རི་ངོས་ཡངས་བྱ་བ་དེ་ཡིན་ཞིང་འོད་སྲུང་ལ་སོགས་དགྲ་བཅོམ་ལྔ་བརྒྱས་བཀའ་བསྡུ་དང་པོ་མཛད་པའི་བྲག་ཕུག་ཀྱང་ཆུ་ཚན་གྱི་ཐག་ཉེ་ལ་ཡོད། ཆུ་ཚན་གྱི་རི་ [༡༢] དེའི་ཁ་ཐུག་བྱང་ངོས་ན་ཡོད་པའི་རི་དེ་རི་བོ་སྐྱ་བསངས་བྱ་བ་དེ་ཡིན་ཞིང་རི་འདི་གཉིས་ཀྱི་མཚམས་དེར་སྔོན་གྲོང་ཁྱེར་གྱི་རྒྱལ་སྒོ་ཡོད་པའི་རྟེན་ཤུལ་ཀྱང་ཡོད། ཆུ་ཚན་གྱི་ཐད་ནས་འོངས་པའི་ཆུ་འགྲམ་བྱང་ཕྱོགས་ས་འབུར་མཐོ་བའི་ཕྱོགས་ཞིག་ཡོད་ས་དེ་(བེ་ལུ་བ་ན་)འོད་མའི་ཚལ་གྱི་ཤུལ་ཡིན་ཞིང་དེར་སྟོན་པ་ལོ་ཤས་བཞུགས། རིའི་ནང་ཕྱོགས་ཀྱི་ཐང་གི་གཡས་གཡོན་ནས་འོངས་པའི་ལྷོ་ཕྱོགས་ཀྱི་ཆུ་ཕྲན་དེ་བརྒྱུད་དེ་ཡར་སོང་ན་ནག་པོ་བརྩེགས་པའི་རི་ཡོད་ཅིང་དེའི་མདུན་གྱི་ཐང་གི་ནགས་ཚལ་དེ་ཤི་ཏ་བ་ན་བྱ་བ་མདོ་ལས་གསུངས་པའི་བསིལ་བ་ཚལ་ཡིན། སྟོན་པ་གཡཱ་མགོ་རི་ནས་རྒྱལ་པོའི་ཁབ་ཏུ་བྱོན་པའི་སྐབས་བསིལ་བ་ཚལ་དེར་ཞག་གཅིག་བཞུགས་ཤིང་རྒྱལ་པོ་གཟུགས་ཅན་སྙིང་པོ་(བིམྦི་ས་ར་)འོངས་ནས་ཐོག་མར་མཇལ། རྒྱལ་པོའི་ཁབ་ཀྱི་བྱང་ངོས་ལ་གིཛྫ་ཀཱུ་ཏེ་བྱ་བ་བྱ་རྒོད་ཕུང་པོའི་རི་བོ་ཡོད་ཅིང་དེ་ནི་སྟོན་པས་ཡུམ་གྱི་མདོ་གསུངས་པའི་གནས་ཡིན། བྱ་རྒོད་ཕུང་པོའི་མདུན་གྱི་ཐང་དུ་(སུམ་གྷི་)མ་གྷ་བཟང་མོའི་རྫིང་བུའི་ཤུལ་ཡོད་ཅིང་དེ་ནས་མར་ལ་འབབ་པའི་ཆུ་དེ་ལ་(སར་སྭ་ཏི་)དབྱངས་ཅན་མའི་ཆུ་ཞེས་གྲགས་སོ།

[X]

གཱ་ཡ་ནས་ཝ་ར་ཎཱ་སི་ལ་འགྲོ་ དེང་སང་གི་མིང་བེ་ན་ར་ས་(BENARAS)ཞེས་ཟེར། གྲོང་ཁྱེར་དེ་ནི་རྒྱ་གར་གྲོང་ཁྱེར་ཀུན་ལས་རྙིང་ཤོས་སུ་གྲགས་ཤིང་བེ་ཤྭ་ན་ཐ་བྱ་བའི་ཕྱི་རོལ་པའི་ལྷ་ཁང་[༡༣]གྲགས་ཅན་དེ་ཡང་དེ་ན་ཡོད། གྲོང་ཁྱེར་ནས་རི་ལ་ལི་ཞུགས་ཏེ་ཅུང་ཟད་སོང་ན་ས་ར་ན་ཐ་(SARNATH)ལ་སླེབས།

and that hill where the hot springs exist is known as the Broad-Flanked Bēpūla (Vipulapārśva) hill from among the five hills of Rājagṛha. And, a short distance from the hot springs there is also a rock cavern where five hundred Arhats, including Kāśyapa, held the first [Buddhist] council. The hill which is to the north, facing that hill with the hot springs **[12]**, is the one known as Mount Pāṇḍu (Pāṇḍugiri) and at a pl. .e between both these hills there also exists a ruined wall wnich had the royal gates to the ancient city in it. That site with ruins, up towards the elevated ground on the north bank of the river which runs directly in front of the hot springs, is the remains of the Bamboo Grove (Veṇuvana), and the Teacher resided there for a few years. If one ascends by way of the southern branch of the stream which run from the left and the right of the plain among the hills, there is the hill of Black Crag (Kālaśilā). The forest on the plain in front of it is the [place we Tibetans call] Cool Grove, which is mentioned in the *sūtra*-s as Śītavana. On the occasion the Teacher went from Gayāśīrṣa to Rājagṛha he dwelt there for a day at the Cool Grove, and when king Bimbisāra arrived there they met for the first time. To the north of Rājagṛha is the Hill of Vulture Heap [as it is called in Tibetan], known as Gṛdhrakūṭa[parvata], and that is the place where the Teacher delivered the *Prajñāpāramitā-sūtra*. On the plain which is in front of Vulture Heap there are the ruins of Sumāgadhā's pool, and the river which flows down from that is renowned as the river of Sarasvatī.

[X. Vārāṇasī and Sārnāth]

From Gayā one goes to Vārāṇasī. Nowadays it is named [and pronounced] "Bi-na-ra-sa" (BENARES). Concerning that city, it is renowned as the oldest of all Indian cities and there is also that famous **[13]** non-Buddhist temple known as Viśvanāth there. Taking the train from the city, and having gone a short distance, one arrives at [the station pronounced] "Sa-ra-na-tha" (SARNATH).

དེ་ནི་དྲང་སྲོང་[༡༣] ལྷུང་བ་རི་དྭ་ཀྱི་ནགས་ཚལ་བྱ་བ་སྟོན་པས་དང་པོར་ཆོས་ཀྱི་འཁོར་ལོ་བསྐོར་བའི་གནས་ཡིན། དེར་སྔོན་གྱི་དགོན་ཆེན་ཆགས་པའི་ཤུལ་དང་ཆོས་འཁོར་བསྐོར་བའི་ས་མིག་དེར་མཆོད་རྟེན་ཆུང་དུ་རྡོའི་དྲ་[༡༤] མིག་གིས་བསྐོར་བ་ཞིག་དང་དེའི་མདུན་ན་ཆོས་རྒྱལ་མྱ་ངན་མེད་ཀྱིས་བཞེངས་པའི་མཆོད་རྟེན་ཆེན་པོ་ཞིག་ཡོད་པ་ད་ལྟའི་ལོ་བརྒྱ་ཕྲག་ཙམ་གྱི་སྔོན་ལ་ཕ་ར་ཊཱ་སིའི་བློན་པོ་སྡིག་ཅན་གྱིས་བཤིག་སྟེ་ཁང་རྡོ་ལ་འཁྱེར་བ་དེའི་ཤུལ་ཡོད། དེ་དང་ཉེ་བ་ན་ཆོས་རྒྱལ་མྱ་ངན་མེད་ཀྱི་རྡོ་རིང་ཆག་གྲུམ་ཞིག་ཡོད་པ་དེའི་སྟེང་གི་ཡི་གེ་དེ་རྣམས་ལོ་ཉིས་སྟོང་ལྷག་པའི་སྔོན་གྱི་རྒྱ་གར་གྱི་ཡི་གེ་ཡིན། ཕྱུར་ངོས་སུ་རྡོའི་མཆོད་རྟེན་ཤིན་ཏུ་ཆེན་པོ་ཞིག་ཡོད་པ་དེ་ཧྨི་ཀའི་མཆོད་རྟེན་བྱ་བ་ཡིན་ཅིང་གུཔྟའི་རྒྱལ་བརྒྱུད་ཀྱི་སྐབས་སུ་བཞེངས། གྲུ་ཟན་ནས་ཡར་འོངས་པའི་ལམ་ཟུར་གྱི་མཆོད་རྟེན་ཞིག་པོ་དེ་ཅོ་ཀན་དེའི་མཆོད་རྟེན་བྱ་བ་འཁོར་ལྔ་སྡེས་སྟོན་པ་དང་པོར་མཇལ་བའི་ས་ཡིན་ཟེར་ཞིང་རྫུའི་ཁང་བུ་དེ་ནི་ཀླ་ཀློ་རྣམས་ཀྱིས་བྱས།

[XI]

དེ་ཡང་རང་རེའི་ཡུལ་དུ་ཀུན་མཁྱེན་བུ་སྟོན་བཞུགས་པའི་དུས་ཙམ་ནས་ཡུལ་དབུས་སུ་བསྟན་པ་ལྷག་མེད་དུ་ཞིག་ཏེ་ལོ་འདི་སྙེད་སོང་ཞིང་། དེ་དག་གི་སྐབས་སུ་ཕྱིར་རྒྱ་གར་ན་བོ་ཧྥི་གཱ་ཡ་ཙམ་ [༡༤] ལས་གནས་གཞན་རྣམས་གར་ཡོད་ཀྱི་མིང་ཙམ་ཡང་མི་ཤེས་ཤིང་། །ཕྱི་བྲག་ཏུ་ཕྱོགས་འདིར་ཡང་ལོ་དྲུག་ཅུ་ཙམ་གྱི་སྔོན་དུ་མུ་སྟེ་ཀ་གཅེར་བུ་པའི་ལྷ་ཁང་ཞིག་ལས་གཞན་ཅི་ཡང་མེད་ཅིང་། ད་ལྟའི་དགོན་ཤུལ་འདི་དག་ཀྱང་ཕག་འཚོ་པའི་ཞིང་དུ་བྱས་ཏེ། མཐའ་ན་ཆོས་འཁོར་བསྐོར་བའི་གནས་ཡིན་པ་ཙམ་ཡང་ཤེས་དཀའ་བར་གྱུར་བ་ན།

[༡༣]) *Orig.* སོང་།

[༡༤]) *Orig.* ཏྲ།

There, in the Ṛṣipatana Deer Park (Ṛṣipatanamṛgadāva), is the holy place where the Teacher first turned the wheel of Buddhist doctrine. Here there are traces of the foundations of a great, ancient monastery, a small funerary monument encircled by stone railings at the exact spot where the wheel of Buddhist doctrine was [first] turned and, in front of that, a large funerary monument which was built by the Buddhist monarch Aśoka. About a century ago it was demolished by an evil minister of Vārāṇasī and the stones taken away for houses.[31] The remains of it are there. Close by to them, there is a fragment of a stone pillar of the Buddhist monarch Aśoka. The lettering on its surface is an Indian script more than two thousand years old. On its near side there is a very large stone funerary monument. That is known as the funerary monument of Dhamek and it was built at the time of the Gupta dynasty. That ruined funerary monument to the side of the road which leads up from the station is known as the funerary monument of Caukhaṇḍī. It is said to be the spot where the Teacher was first met by the Group of Five disciples,[32] and the building at its top was made by the barbarians (i.e. the Mughals).[33]

[XI. Dharmapāla's Works at Sārnāth]

Furthermore, since about the time when the polymath Butön (1290-1364) lived in our land, the Buddhist teachings have been completely eradicated in the Middle Country (Madhyadeśa), and so many years have elapsed. During that period, in India generally, apart from Bodh Gayā **[14]** even the names of where other holy places had existed were unknown. In this region [of Sārnāth] in particular, even a mere sixty years ago there was nothing whatsoever other than a temple of the naked heretics (i.e. Jains), and the ruins of the monastery also [seen here] today were used as a field for rearing swine. Finally, when it became difficult to know even that this was the holy place of the [first] turning of the wheel of Buddhist doctrine,

ལྷོ་ཕྱོགས་སིནྡྷལའི་གླིང་ནས་སྐྱེས་བུ་སྙིང་སྟོབས་ཀྱི་བདག་ཉིད་ཆེན་པོ་དགེ་བསྙེན་རྣམ་པཱ་ལ་བྱ་བ་བྱོན་ཏེ། ལུས་སྲོག་ཡོངས་སྤྱོད་ལ་མ་ལྟོས་པའི་དཀའ་བ་བརྒྱ་ཕྲག་གི་སྒོ་ནས། དྲང་སྲོང་སྨྲ་བ་རི་དྭགས་ཀྱི་ནགས་ཚལ་འདིར་གཙུག་ལག་ཁང་དང་མཧཱ་བོ་དྷིའི་ཚོགས་བཙུགས། སིནྡྷལའི་གླིང་ནས་འདུལ་ཆོག་སྡེ་གསུམ་ཚང་བའི་དགེ་འདུན་སྤྱན་དྲངས་ཏེ། སྐར་ཡང་ཡུལ་དབུས་མ་ག་དྷ་ན་ཤཱཀྱའི་དགེ་སློང་སྣམ་སྦྱར་གྱི་རྒྱལ་མཚན་གྱོན་པ་རྣམས་མིག་གིས་མཐོང་བར་གྱུར་ཅིང་། དེ་མཚུངས་རྡོ་རྗེ་གདན་ཀ་ལི་ཀ་ཏ་ཕྱི་གླིང་[༡༥]གི་རྒྱལ་ས་ལོ་ཊོན་རྣམས་སུ་ཡང་གཙུག་ལག་ཁང་དང་དགེ་འདུན་གྱི་སྡེ་བཙུགས་ཏེ། སྐར་ཡང་རྒྱ་གར་དུ་བསྟན་པ་ཕྱི་དར་གྱི་མགོ་བརྩམས་སོ།

དེ་ལྟ་བུའི་བདག་ཉིད་ཆེན་པོ་དེས་རང་གིས་ཁུར་དུ་བྱས་པའི་བྱ་བ་དག་མཐར་ཕྱིན་པར་བྱས་ཤིང་། དུས་ཀྱི་མཇུག་ཏུ་རང་ཉིད་ཀྱང་ཁྱིམ་ནས་ཁྱིམ་མེད་པར་རབ་ཏུ་བྱུང་སྟེ་གཙུག་ལག་ཁང་འདི་ཉིད་དུ་ [༡༥] བཞུགས་ཤིང་འཁོར་ལོ་གཉིས་ཀྱི་བྱ་བ་ལ་བརྩོན་བཞིན་པའི་ངང་ནས་སྐུ་ཚེའི་འདུ་བྱེད་རྫོགས་ཏེ་ད་ལྟའི་མི་གླང་འདི་བར་ལོ་ངོ་ལྔ་སོང་།

དེས་བཞེངས་པའི་མཱུ་ལ་གན་དྷ་ཀུ་ཊིའི་གཙུག་ལག་ཁང་འདིར་སངས་རྒྱས་ཀྱི་སྐུ་རུས་ཚན་པ་གཉིས་ཡོད་པའི་གཅིག་ནི་རྡོ་འཛིག་ཡུལ་གྱི་མཆོད་རྟེན་རྙིང་པ་ཞིག་ལས་ཐོབ་ཅིང་། གཅིག་ནི་ལྷོ་ཕྱོགས་དཔལ་གྱི་རི་ནས་རྙེད་པ་སྟེ་རིན་པོ་ཆེའི་ག་བུ་དང་རྡོ་སྒྲོམ་དུ་བཙུག་པའི་ཕྱི་ལ་འདི་སངས་རྒྱས་སྐུ་རུས་ཡིན་ནོ་བྱ་བའི་ལོ་ཉིས་སྟོང་གི་སྔོན་དུས་ཀྱི་ཡི་གེ་བཏབ་པ་བཅས་རྙེད་པས་ཤིན་ཏུ་འཁྲུལ་མེད་ཡིན་ནོ། སྐུ་རུས་དེ་རྒྱུན་དུ་སྟོན་པའི་སྐུ་བརྙན་གྱི་བཞུགས་ཁྲིའི་ནང་དུ་བཞུགས་ཤིང་། ལོ་རེ་བཞིན་ཕྱི་གླིང་གི་ཟླ་བ་བཅུ་གཅིག་པའི་ནང་འཆར་ཅན་གྱི་ཚེས་བཅོ་ལྔའི་ཟླ་བ་ཉ་གང་བ་ན་ཕྱི་རོལ་དུ་སྤྱན་དྲངས་ཏེ་དངོས་སུ་མཇལ་ཐུབ་ཅིང་།

༡༥) *Orig.* ཀླིང་།

there arrived from the southern island of Ceylon (Siṃhaladvīpa) the person of the courageous great soul (*mahātman*), the Buddhist layman known as Dharmapāla. By way of a hundred difficulties and without regard for life and property, he founded a monastic centre and the Maha Bodhi Society here at the Ṛṣivadana Deer Park (Ṛṣivadanamṛgadāva). From Ceylon he invited monks completely versed in the three divisions of the *Vinaya* and, in the Middle Country, Magadha, fully ordained Buddhist monks clothed with the victory banner of the monastic outer robe became seen once again. Like that, monastic centres and communities of Buddhists were founded also at Vajrāsana, Calcutta, the capitals of Europe, and London, and thereafter the beginnings of the later diffusion of the Buddhist teachings in India was accomplished.

Because he was such a great man, [Dharmapāla] brought to completion the works which he had undertaken, and at the end of this period he himself also renounced the householder's life, became ordained, and resided **[15]** in this very monastic centre [here at Sārnāth]. He completed his life's cyclic existence with a characteristic exertion in the two spheres [of teaching and maintaining the Buddhist doctrine], since which five years have elapsed up until this present [Tibetan year] of the fire-ox (=1937).

Of the two sets of the Buddha's bone relics[34] in this Mūlagandhakuṭī monastic centre which [the Maha Bodhi Society] erected [here at Sārnāth], one of them was obtained from an ancient funerary monument in the country of Taxila.[35] The other one was discovered at Śrī Parvata to the south,[36] and because it was found placed in a stone casket, with precious stones,[37] the outside of which had a two thousand year old inscription stating "This is the Buddha's bone", there is absolutely no disputing that it is.[38] That bone always resides within the throne of the statue of the Teacher, and every year on the full moon of the fifteenth day [of the Tibetan lunar calendar], usually during the eleventh Western [calendar] month, it is invited outside and one can obtain a direct encounter with it.[39]

ཕྱོགས་ཀྱི་གནས་བསྐོར་བ་རྣམས་སྟོད་སའི་མགྲོན་ཁང་ཁྱིམ་བདག་ཆེན་པོ་འབེར་ལས་རྒྱབ་པ་དང་། གཞན་སེནྣ་ལ་དང་དྷར་མའི་དྷརྨཔཱལ་བཅས་ཡོད་དོ།

[XII]

ས་ར་ན་ཐའི་གྲུ་ཟན་ནས་ཊེ་ཀ་བླངས་ཏེ་ཏ་སིལ་དེ་བོ་རི་ཡ་བར་དང་དེ་ནས་མོ་ཊར་ནས་ཀུ་ཤི་ན་ར་ལ་སླེབས། དེ་ནི་རྩ་མཆོག་གྲོང་ཡིན་ཅིང་དེང་སང་མིང་ལ་མ་ཐ་ཀུ་ཨར་ཟེར། རྒྱ་གར་ཤར་ཕྱོཊ་ན་ཡང་རྩ་མཆོག་གྲོང་སོགས་ཡོད་ཅིང་། ནུབ་ཕྱོགས་ཨ་ཕ་ཀ་ནི་སཏན་ [༡༨] དུ་ཡང་སྐུ་འབྲུངས་པ་ ཆོས་འཁོར་བསྐོར་བ་མྱ་ངན་འདས་པའི་གནས་ཐམས་ཅད་ཡོད་ཅིང་། དེ་བཞིན་ཡུལ་གྲུ་གཞན་མང་པོར་ཡང་ཡོད་མོད། སྟོན་པ་རང་ཉིད་གདུལ་བྱ་ཐུན་མོང་གི་ངོར་མྱ་ངན་ལས་འདས་པའི་གནས་ནི་ཡུལ་དབུས་ཀྱི་འདི་ཉིད་འབྲུལ་མེད་ཡིན་ནོ། དྷར་མས་བཞེངས་པའི་གསེར་གྱི་མཆོད་རྟེན་གྱི་ཤར་མེ་ལི་གཅིག་ལྷག་ཙམ་ན་མཆོད་རྟེན་ཞིག་པོ་ཨམྲའི་[༡༨] སྟོང་པོ་སྐྲུས་པ་ཞིག་ཡོད་པ་དེ་མུ་ཀུཊབན་དྷ་ན་བྱ་བའི་མཆོད་རྟེན་ཏེ་སྐུ་གདུང་ཞུགས་ལ་བཞུས་པའི་གནས་ཡིན་ཅིང་དེང་སང་གི་མིང་ལ་ར་མ་བྷར་ཞེས་ཟེར། དེ་ཀྱང་ཀྱིས་དབུ་རྒྱན་བཅིང་བའི་མཆོད་རྟེན་ཞེས་མདོ་ལས་འབྱུང་བ་དེ་ལགས།

[XIII]

རྩ་མཆོག་གྲོང་ནས་མོ་ཊར་ལས་གོ་རག་པུར་ལ་འགྲོ་གྲོང་ཁྱེར་དེའི་མཐའ་ན་གོ་རག་ན་ཐ་ཕན་བྱ་བའི་ལྷ་ཁང་ཞིག་ཡོད་པ་དེ་གྲུབ་ཐོབ་བརྒྱད་ཅུའི་ནང་གི་གོ་རཀྵའི་བཞུགས་གནས་ཡིན་ཟེར་ཅིང་། གྲུབ་ཆེན་དེའི་ཆོས་བརྒྱུད་ཕྱི་རོལ་པའི་ལུགས་དང་བསྲེས་ནས་འཛིན་པ་རྣ་བ་ལ་ཨ་ལོང་ཆེན་པོ་བཏགས་པའི་སྡེ་ཚན་དེ་དག་ཡིན་ཅིང་ད་དུང་གྲུབ་ཆེན་དེའི་དོ་ཧ་ཡང་འདོན་པར་བྱེད།

---

༡༨) *Orig.* ཨམྲིའི།

There is a guest-house to accommodate pilgrims at the site, which was made by the great citizen Birla,[40] together with other Sinhalese and Burmese pilgrims rest-houses.

[XII. Kuśinagarī]

Purchasing a ticket from the Sārnāth station as far as Tahsil-Deoria, and from there by motorcar, one reaches Kuśinagarī. That is Tsamchogdrong [in Tibetan], and its name today is Māthākuwar. In eastern India there is another Kuśinagarī, and to the west in Afghanisthan **[16]** also there are all the holy places where [the Buddha] took birth, turned the wheel of Buddhist doctrine and passed beyond suffering, and thus they also exist in many other lands. In the view of the common convert, the holy place where the Teacher himself passed beyond suffering is indisputably this very one in the Middle Country. Over a mile to the east of the golden funerary monument which was built by the Burmese, there is a ruined funerary monument with a mango tree growing there. That funerary monument is known as Mukundānanda, and it is the holy place where the cremation of [Buddha's] remains took place and which today has the name Rāmābhār. It is that which is mentioned in a *sūtra* as "The funerary monument to which the Malla bound a diadem."

[XIII. Gorakhpur]

From Kuśinagarī one goes to Gorakhpur by motorcar. At the edge of that town there is a temple known as Gorakhnātha-phana. It is said that was a dwelling place of Gorakṣa [i.e. Gorakhnāth], who was one of the eighty Tantric adepts. The Buddhist doctrinal lineage of that great Tantric adept was mixed with that of the non-Buddhist [Nāth] sect, being those orders whose adherents wear large rings in their ears and who still also recite the Tantric songs of that great Tantric adept.

[XIV]

གོ་རག་པུར་ནས་རེལ་ལི་ཞུགས་ནས་ནའོ་ཏན་པ་དང་དེ་ནས་མེ་ལི་བདུན་བརྒྱད་ཙམ་སོང་པས་ལིཙྪི་ཝི་ལ་སླེབས་དེང་སང་མིང་ལ་ཧུ་མན་དེ་ཞེས་ཟེར། དེ་ནི་སྟོན་པ་སྐུ་འཁྲུངས་པའི་གནས་ཡིན་ཅིང་། [༡༧] དེར་སྒྱུ་འཕྲུལ་མའི་སྐུ་བརྙན་དང་། ཆོས་རྒྱལ་མྱ་ངན་མེད་ཀྱི་རྡོ་རིང་ལ་རྒྱལ་པོ་ཁྲི་ལོ་ཉེར་གཅིག་པར་ཕྱོགས་དེར་སླེབས་ནས། ཕྱོགས་འདིར་སངས་རྒྱས་འཁྲུངས་སོ། ཞེས་རྡོ་རིང་བསླང་བ་ཡིན་བྱ་བའི་ཡི་གེ་ཅན་ཡོད། ལིཙྪིབིའི་ནུབ་ཕྱོགས་མེ་ལི་ལྔ་དྲུག་ཙམ་ན་—(ཀཔིལབསྟུ་) སེར་སྐྱའི་གྲོང་ཁྱེར་གྱི་ཤུལ་ཡོད་ཅིང་དེང་སང་གི་མིང་ལ་ཧི་ལོ་ར་ཀོ་ཊ་ཟེར་དེ་ནས་མེ་ལི་གཅིག་ཙམ་ན་དིག་ལི་ཕ་བྱ་བར་སངས་རྒྱས་འཁོར་བ་འཇིག་གི་ཁྲིན་པ་སྟོན་གྱི་ཁ་བྱང་བཏབ་པ་ཡོད།

[XV]

དེ་ནས་སྦྱར་གྱི་རེལ་ལི་ནས་ཕ་རེན་ད་དང་དེ་ནས་ཊེ་ཀ་ཉོས་ཧེ་བལ་རམ་པུར་བར་འགྲོ བལ་རམ་པུར་ནས་མེ་ལི་བཅུ་ཙམ་སོང་ན་མཉན་ཡོད་(ཤྲཱཝསྟི་)ལ་སླེབས་དེང་སང་གི་མིང་ལ་ས་ཧེ་ཊ་མ་ཧེད་ཟེར། ཧྲར་མའི་རྣམ་སྣ་ལ་དང་ཉེ་བ་ན་རྒྱལ་བུ་རྒྱལ་བྱེད་ཀྱི་ཚལ་(ཛེ་ཏ་བ་ན་)མགོན་མེད་ཟས་སྦྱིན་གྱི་ཀུན་དགའ་ར་བའི་ཤུལ་ཡོད་ཅིང་། དེར་སངས་རྒྱས་རང་ཉིད་བཞུགས་པའི་གཙུག་ལག་ཁང་ ༡ རྣཛ་ཀུ་ཊི། ༢ ཀོཾ་ཤམྦིའི་ཀུ་ཊི། ༣ ཀཀེ་རི་ཀོ་ཊི། ༤ གན་དྷ་ཀུ་ཊི། (དྲི་གཙང་ཁང་) བཞི་ཀའི་ཤུལ་ཡོད། དེ་ལ་གན་དྷ་ཀུ་ཊི་ནི་སྟོན་པ་བཞུགས་པའི་གཟིམ་སྤྱིལ་གཙོ་བོ་ཡིན་ཞིང་། སྤྱིར་མཉན་ཡོད་འདི་ནི་སྟོན་པའི་བཞུགས་གནས་ཀུན་གྱི་ནང་ནས་གཙོ་བོ་ཡིན་ཏེ། རྒྱལ་བྱེད་[༡༨] ཚལ་རང་ལ་དབྱར་ཉི་ཤུ་དང་། རི་དྭགས་འཛིན་གྱི་མའི་ཤར་གྱི་ཀུན་དགའ་ར་བར་དབྱར་ལྔ་སྟེ་ཁྲིན་[༡༧] བསྡོམ་པས་ལོ་ཉི་ཤུ་རྩ་ལྔ་བཞུགས།

༡༧) *Orig.* འཁྲིན།

[XIV. Lumbinī]

Going by rail from Gorakhpur to Nautanwa, and then by proceeding some seven or eight miles from there, one arrives at Lumbinī. Today its name is Rummindei. That is the holy place where the Teacher took birth, and **[17]** in that place there is a statue of [the Buddha's mother] Māyā and a stone pillar of the Buddhist monarch Aśoka on which is found an inscription stating: "The king arrived here in the twenty-first year of his reign," then: "The Buddha was born here", and that he erected the stone pillar.[41] Some five or six miles to the west of Lumbinī there are the ruins of the city of Serkya [as it is known in Tibetan], Kapilavastu, and today it has the name Tilaurakot.[42] About one mile from there, in the place called Nigliva, there is a well of the [former] Buddha Krakucchanda with an ancient inscription.[43]

[XV. Śrāvastī]

From there, with the train as before, one goes to Pharenda and from there one buys a ticket to Balrāmpur. If one proceeds about ten miles from Balrāmpur, one reaches Śrāvastī. Today it is named Saheṭh-Maheṭh. Close by to the Burmese pilgrims rest-house there is the Jetavana, [known in Tibetan as] the Gyalbu Gyalchekyi Tsel, with the ruins of Anāthapiṇḍada's Pleasure Garden (Anāthapiṇḍadārāma), and in that place are the ruins of four monastic centres where the Buddha himself resided: i. Rājakuṭī; ii. Kauśāmbīkuṭī; iii. Kakerikuṭī; iv. Gandhakuṭī [which translated in Tibetan is] Dritsangkhang. As for Gandhakuṭī, it was the principal sleeping hut in which the Teacher resided and, in general, from among all of the Teacher's dwelling places this site of Śrāvastī was the main one. **[18]** He spent twenty-five years here all together, with twenty rainy seasons at Jetavana itself and five rainy seasons at the Eastern Pleasure Garden (Pūrvārāma) of Mṛgāramātar.

མཆོག་ཟུང་གཉིས། ལྷ་སྡེ་བཟང་པོ། གནས་བརྟན་བཅུ་དྲུག་འོད་སྲུང་འཆར་ཀ། ཧ་ཐུལ་ལ་སོགས་པ་སྟོན་པའི་འཁོར་གྱི་གཙོ་བོ་ཉན་ཐོས་ཆེན་པོ་བརྒྱད་ཅུ་ཞེས་གྲགས་པ་དེ་ཀུན་ཀྱང་ཕལ་ཆེར་གནས་འདིར་ཡུན་རིང་བཞུགས་པ་ཤ་སྟག་ཡིན། སངས་རྒྱས་ཀྱིས་ཆོ་འཕྲུལ་ཆེན་མོ་བསྟན་པའི་གནས་ཀྱང་འདི་ཡིན། རྒྱལ་བྱེད་ཚལ་ནས་བྱང་དུ་བལྟས་ན་སོ་ཕག་གི་ལྕུགས་རི་ཞིག་པོ་སྣང་བརྒྱུད་ལྟ་བུ་མཐོང་པ་དེ་མཉན་ཡོད་དུ་ཡོད་པའི་གྲོང་ཁྱེར་གྱི་ཤུལ་ཡིན་ཅིང་དེའི་ཤར་ངོས་ན་གྲོང་ཐོར་རེ་བ་ཞིག་མཐོང་པ་དེ་ཤར་གྱི་ཀུན་དགའ་ར་བའི་ཤུལ་ཡིན་ནམ་ཟེར། དེས་ན་མཉན་ཡོད་འདི་ནི་རང་རེ་སངས་རྒྱས་པ་ཀུན་གྱིས་མཐོང་ན་སྟོན་པའི་མཛད་སྤྱོད་ཀུན་ལ་དྲན་གསོས་ཐེབས་[༡༨] པའི་གནས་ཡིན་མོད་གནས་སྐོར་བ་རྣམས་ཨམ་འབབ་སར་ལ་འགྲོ་བའི་ལམ་ནས་གཡས་བསྐྱུར་གཡོན་བསྐྱུར་བྱས་ཏེ་འགྲོ་བ་འདི་བློ་ཕམ་ཆེ།

[XVI]

སླར་བལ་རམ་པུར་ནས་ཏེ་ཀ་གླངས་ཏེ་ལག་ཉོ་དང་དེ་ནས་པ་ཁ་ན་བར་དང་དེ་ནས་མེ་ལི་འགའ་ཙམ་སོང་ན་སང་ཁ་ས་ལ་སླེབས། དེ་ནི་སྟོན་པ་ཡུམ་ལ་ཆོས་གསུངས་པའི་སྐད་དུ་ལྷ་ཡུལ་དུ་དབྱར་གཅིག་བཞུགས་ཤིང་སླར་འཛམ་གླིང་དུ་བབས་པའི་གནས་ཡིན། [༡༩] དེར་སྔོན་བཙུན་པ་ཐང་ཟན་གྱིས་གཟིགས་པའི་མྱ་ངན་མེད་ཀྱི་རྡོ་རིང་གི་ཏོག་གླང་ཆེན་གྱི་གཟུགས་ཞིག་ས་མིག་ལྟ་བུར་ཡོད།

དེ་ལྟར་གོང་དུ་བཤད་པའི་གནས་འདི་དག་ནི་ཡོངས་སུ་གྲགས་པའི་གནས་ཆེན་རྣམས་ཀྱི་གཙོ་བོ་ཡིན་ཅིང་རེ་ལ་ལི་བརྒྱད་ན་ཕན་ཚུན་དེ་ཙམ་གྱི་ཐག་རིང་ཀྱང་མེན་པས་ཅིས་ཀྱང་མཇལ་ཐུབ་པ་ལ་འབད་པར་བྱའོ།

---

༡༨) *Orig.* ཐེབ།

Also, all those renowned ones known as the Eighty Great Śrāvaka, the chief disciples of the Teacher, including the Superior Pair,[44] the good Group of Five, the Sixteen Elders, Kāśyapa, Udāyi and Aśvajit, for the most part all dwelt for long periods at this holy place. This is also the holy place at which the Buddha displayed great miracles. If one looks north from Jetavana, that ruined brick perimeter wall one sees resembling a series of hillocks is the remains of the city which existed at Śrāvastī, and on its eastern side that individual dwelling one sees is the remains of the Eastern Pleasure Garden, or so it is said. Thus, when Buddhists behold Śrāvastī here for themselves, it is a holy place which rekindles the memory of all the deeds accomplished by the Teacher. There are pilgrims who strike out to the right and the left of the road which goes to Amritsar, and these [side] trips are very disappointing.

[XVI. Sāṃkāśya]

Once again, one purchases a ticket from Balrāmpur to Lucknow, and from there as far as Pakhna, and if one goes just a few miles on from there one arrives at Sāṃkāśya. The Teacher spent one rainy season in the [Trayastriṃśa] heaven in order to preach the Buddhist doctrine to his mother, and this is the holy place where he descended to the Southern Continent once again. **[19]** The figure of an elephant, which was the capital of an Aśokan stone pillar seen here in the past by the [Chinese] monk Hsüan-tsang, exists here as if it was the exact spot [he visited].[45]

As for those sites which are explained above, they are paramount among the great holy places which are universally famous. To the extent to which they are connected by the railway system, they are not far distant [from one another], therefore by all means make the effort to obtain a direct encounter with them!

[XVII]

བེ་ན་ར་སི་ནས་ཨ་ལ་ཧ་བ་ད་དང་དེ་ནས་ཕྷར་ཕ་རི་བར་སོང་ནས་མོ་ཊར་ལམ་མེ་ལི་མང་ཙམ་སོང་བ་ན་ཆུ་བོ་ཡ་མུ་ནའི་འགྲམ་དུ་ཀཽ་ཤམྦིའི་ཤུལ་ཡོད་དེང་སང་ཡང་ཀཽ་ཤམ་ཟེར་དེར་མྱ་ངན་མེད་ཀྱི་རྡོ་རིང་དང་ཞིང་གི་དཀྱིལ་ན་སྔོན་གྱི་གྲོང་ཁྱེར་གྱི་ལྷ་ཊ་རི་གསལ་ཙམ་ཡོད། འདིར་བློན་པོ་གདངས་ཅན་གྱིས་སངས་རྒྱས་སྤྱན་དྲངས་ཏེ་ལོ་གཅིག་བཞུགས། ཀཽ་ཤམྦི་ནས་ལྷོ་ཕྱོགས་རྒྱང་རིང་པོ་ན་རི་བོ་འབིགས་བྱེད་ཀྱང་གསལ་བར་མཐོང་།

[XVIII]

ཡང་བེ་ན་ར་སི་ནས་ཕེ་ཟ་བ་ད་དང་དེ་ནས་ཆུ་བོ་ས་ར་ཡུའི་ལྷོ་འགྲམ་དུ་ཨ་ཡོདྷྱ་ཡོད། དེ་ནི་གྲོང་ཁྱེར་འཐབ་པ་མེད་པ་རྒྱལ་པོ་དགའ་བྱེད་རྭ་མ་འཁྲུངས་པའི་གནས་ཡིན་ཅིང་གྲོང་ཁྱེར་དྲུག་གི་ནང་ཚན་ས་ཀེཏ་(གནས་བཅས་)ཡང་དེ་ཡིན། ཨ་ལ་ཧ་བ་ད་ནས་ཌྷེ་ལི་ལ་འགྲོ་བའི་ལམ་དུ་ཐོག་མར་ཨག་ར་བྱ་བར་སླེབས། དེར་[༡༠] ཀླ་ཀློའི་རྒྱལ་པོ་ཤ་ཛཧན་གྱི་བཙུན་མོའི་(མཛེས་མ་མུཾ་ཏ་ཛེ་)རོ་ཁང་འཛིག་རྟེན་ན་གྲགས་པ་དེ་ཡོད། བྱིན་རླབས་ནི་བཤད་རྒྱུ་མེད་ལ། ངོ་མཚར་ནི་བཤད་ན་མི་འཛད་པས་འདིར་མ་བྲིས།

[XIX]

ཨག་ར་ནས་སོང་ན་མ་ཐུ་ར་ལ་སླེབས་དེ་ནི་བཅོམ་བརླག་གི་ཡུལ་ཧེ་ད་དུང་ཡང་གྲོང་ཁྱེར་ཆེ། དེར་སྟོན་པ་ཡང་བྱོན་ཅིང་འཕགས་པ་ཤ་ནའི་གོས་ཅན་ཀྱང་ཡུན་རིང་བཞུགས། སྔོན་རྒྱལ་བསྟན་ཤིན་ཏུ་དར་བའི་གནས་ཡིན།

[XVII. Kauśāmbī]

Having gone from Benares to Allahābād, and from there as far as Bharwari, if one goes on for many miles by motorcar there are the ruins of Kauśāmbī[46] on the banks of the river Yamunā (see figure 2). Today it is still called Kosham (i.e. Kosam). There, in the centre of a field with an Aśokan stone pillar, the perimeter wall of the ancient city exists quite clearly. The minister Ghoṣila invited the Buddha here, and he stayed for a year. Far to the south of Kauśāmbī the Vindhya Hills (Vindhyaparvata) are also clearly visible.

[XVIII. Ayodhya and Agra]

Also from Benares [one goes to] Faizābād, and after that on the south bank of the river [Ghāghara, whose ancient name was] Sarayū there is Ayodhya. That peaceable city is the place where joyous Rāma was born, and it was [known as] Sāketā [which in Tibetan is] Néche, one of the six [great] cities [of the Buddha's era]. On the first part of the road which goes from Allahābād to Delhi, one reaches a place called Āgra. Here **[20]** there is that world famous [Taj Mahal], mausoleum for the barbarian (i.e. Mughal) emperor Shāh Jahān's (r.1627-1658) queen, beautiful Mumtāz. Concerning its empowerment [as a Buddhist holy place], there is nothing to explain, and since its marvels cannot be described I will write nothing of it here.[47]

[XIX. Mathurā to Delhi]

If one goes on from Āgra, one arrives in Mathurā. That is the land which [in Tibetan is called] Chomlag, and today it is also a great city. The Buddha went there also, and the exalted Śāṇakavāsin dwelt there a long time as well. In the past this was a place where the Buddha's teachings spread extensively.

དེར་མུ་ཟེམ་(MUSEUM)ཁང་དུ་ཕྱོགས་དེ་ནས་རྙེད་པའི་སྐུ་བརྙན་རྣམས་བཞུགས། བཅོམ་བརླག་གི་བྱང་གནྡྷ་ར་དང་ཡ་མུ་ནའི་བར་གྱི་ཡུལ་དེ་རྣམས་(པཉྩལ་) ལྷོ་ལེན་གྱི་ཡུལ་ཡིན། དེ་ནས་དྷེ་ལི་ལ་སླེབས་ཤིང་ཕྱོགས་དེ་སྔོན་གྱི་ཀུ་རུའི་ཡུལ་ཡིན།

[XX]

དྷེ་ལི་ནས་རེལ་ལི་ཞུགས་ཏེ་ཨམྦ་ལ་དང་ཛ་ལན་དྷ་ར་བརྒྱུད་ནས་ཨམ་ཙྲར་སར་(ཨམྲིཏ་སར་)དུ་སླེབས། ཨམ་ཙྲར་སར་ནི་གུ་རུ་ན་ན་ཀ་དེ་བོའི་གནས་རྣམས་ཀྱི་གཙོ་བོ་ཡིན་ཅིང་། གུ་རུ་དེ་རབ་བྱུང་བརྒྱད་པའི་ས་མོ་གླང་གི་ལོ་ལ་ནུབ་ཕྱོགས་ལ་ཧོར་དང་ཉེ་བའི་གྲོང་ཞིག་ཏུ་ཚོང་དཔོན་ཀ་ལུ་བྱེ་བའི་སྲས་སུ་འཁྲུངས་ཏེ་ད་ལྟའི་མེ་གླང་འདི་བར་ལོ་དྲུག་བརྒྱ་དང་བཞི་སོང་། དགུང་ལོ་བདུན་ཅུ་པ་ལ་སྐུ་གཤེགས་ཤིང་དེའི་རྗེས་གུ་རུའི་ཆོས་བརྒྱུད་འཛིན་པ། རཱ་མ་ [༡༧] ད་ས་དང་། གོ་བིནྡ་སིངྷ་སོགས་གུ་རུ་དགུ་ཙམ་བྱོན། ཁོང་གི་ཆོས་བརྒྱུད་དེ་ལ་སི་ཀ་ཟེར་བ་དེང་སང་སིག་ཏུ་འབོད་པའི་སྐྱེས་པོ་རང་བཞིན་བཟང་ཞིང་སྦྱིན་པ་ལ་དགའ་བ་ནང་པ་དང་ཁྱད་མེད་པ་དེ་དག་བྱུང་བ་ཡིན།

[XXI]

ཨམ་འབར་སར་ནས་པ་ཐན་ཀོ་ཊེ་དང་། དེ་ནས་ནག་རོ་ཊ་བར་རེལ་ལི་འགྲོ་ནག་རོ་ཊར་མ་སླེབས་པའི་གྱ་ཟན་གཉིས་ཀྱི་གོང་དུ་ཀཱང་ར་བྱ་བར་སླེབས། རྒྱའི་བྱང་ཕྱོགས་ཀྱི་རི་ངོས་སུ་གྲོང་ཁྱེར་ཀཱང་ར་ཡོད། དེ་ནི་གནས་ཆེན་ཉེར་བཞིའི་ནང་གི་ནུབ་ཕྱོགས་ཛ་ལན་དྷ་ར་བྱ་བའི་གྲགས་ཆེན་དེ་ཡིན་ཞིང་། རྗེ་རྒོད་ཚང་པ་མགོན་པོ་རྡོ་རྗེ་དང་། དེའི་སློབ་མ་ཨོ་རྒྱན་པ་དང་། སྟག་ཚང་རས་པ། རང་རིག་རས་པ་སོགས་སྔར་ཕྱོགས་འདིར་བྱོན་པ་སོ་སོའི་རྣམ་ཐར་དུ་གསལ།

The MUSEUM there contains statues which were discovered in that area. North of Chomlag, those lands which are between the Gangā and the Yamunā were the [ancient] country of Pañcāla, [which in Tibetan is] Ngalen. From there one arrives in Delhi, and that region was formerly the [ancient] country of Kuru.

[XX. Amritsar]

Taking the train from Delhi, and passing through Ambāla and Jullundur, one arrives at Amritsar. Concerning Amritsar, it was the foremost of Guru Nānak Deva's (1469-1539) abodes. That Guru was born in the earth-female-ox year (=1469) of the eighth sixty year [Tibetan] calendrical cycle, as the son of a leading merchant named Kalu in a town close by to Lahore to the west, and up to this present [year] of the fire-ox (=1937) six hundred and four years have since elapsed.[48] He passed away at seventy years of age, and after that as many as nine gurus appeared, including **[21]** Rām Dās (1574-1581) and Gobind Singh (1675-1708) as holders of the Guru's religious lineage. His religious lineage was called "Si-ka". The people who are named Sikh nowadays are good natured, and it appears they are no different to Buddhists as they enjoy giving alms.

[XXI. Western Himalayan Tantric Sites]

The train goes from Amritsar to Pathānkot and from there as far as Nagrota. Two stations before it reaches Nagrota, one arrives in the place called Kāngra. Kāngra township is on a hillside to the north of the river. From among the twenty-four great Tantric sites, it is that very famous one known as Jālandhara to the west [i.e. of India, conceived as the hypostatic *vajrakāya*], and this is evident in the biographies of individuals who travelled to this region in the past, including the master Götsangpa Gompo Dorje (1189-1258) and his disciple Orgyenpa (1230-1308/9), Tagtsang Repa (1574-1651) and Rangrig Repa.[49]

ལྷག་པར་རྟོད་ཚང་པ་དེ་འདིར་ལོ་ཕྱེད་ཙམ་བཞུ་ཊ་ཤིང་གནས་བཤད་ཞིབ་ཏུ་གསུངས་
པས་ཐེ་ཚོམ་ཐམས་ཅད་ཆོད་པ་ཡོད། མཇལ་ས་གཙོ་བོ་ཀྣང་ར་མན་དེར་ནང་དུ
མགོ་ལྷ་བུའི་ལིངྒ་དེ་ཡིན། ཀྣང་རར་མ་སླེབས་གོང་དུ་ཛྭ་ལ་མུ་ཁི་བྲ་བར་སླེབས།
དེར་ས་ལ་མེ་འབར་མཇལ་རྒྱུ་ཡོད་ཅིང་། དེ་ཡང་རྟོད་ཚང་རྣམ་ཐར་དུ་གསལ།
ནག་རོ་ཊ་ནས་མོ་ཊར་ལ་ཞུགས་ཏེ་མན་དེ་གྲོང་བརྒྱུད་ནས་མཚོ་པདྨ་ར་བལ་སར་
དུ་སླེབས། ཡང་ནམ་དེའི་ཆུ་བརྒྱུད་ནས་མོ་ཊར་ལས་ [༡༡] ཀུ་ལུ་ལ་སླེབས། ཡུལ་
དེ་ལ་བོད་སྐད་དུ་ཉུང་ཏི་ཟེར། དེ་གནས་ཆེན་ཉེར་བཞིའི་ནང་གི་ཀུ་ལུ་ཏ་ཡིན་པར་
གཞུང་མང་པོར་གསུངས་ཤིང་། བུ་སྟོན་གྱི་བདེ་མཆོག་སྤྱི་རྣམ་དུ་གར་ཞའི་རྒྱལ་
ཉུང་ཏིའི་ཕྱུག་ཞེས་ཤིན་ཏུ་གསལ་བར་བཤད། པུས་མོ་ལྷ་བུའི་ལིངྒ་ནི་ཤར་རིའི་
རྩེ་ན་ཡོད་པའི་ལྷ་རྟེན་གློག་གི་དབང་ཕྱུག་(*vijalīśvara*) བྱ་བ་དེ་ཡིན་ཟེར། འོན་
ཀྱང་བུ་སྟོན་གྱིས་བྲག་ཕྱུག་ཞིག་ན་ཡོད་པར་གསུངས། ཀུ་ལུའི་བྱང་དུ་རོ་ཐང་ལ་
བརྒལ་ན་བོད་ཀྱི་ཡུལ་གར་ཞ་མཁའ་འགྲོའི་གླིང་ཞེས་འབྲི་གུང་སྐྱོབ་པས་བསྔགས་
པ་དེར་སླེབས། དེར་དྲིལ་བུ་རི་དང་། ལུང་སྨད་དུ་འཕགས་པ་འཇིག་རྟེན་གསུམ་
མགོན་བྱ་བའི་སྤྱན་རས་གཟིགས་ཀྱི་སྣང་བརྙན་ངོ་མཚར་ཅན་དེ་བཞུགས། འཕགས་
པའི་བཞུགས་ས་ནས་མར་ལ་ཚ་ལམ་ཙམ་གྱི་སར་ཧྨག་བ་ཧི་བྱ་བ་ལྷ་མོ་བགྲོད་དཀའི་
གནས་ཤིན་ཏུ་གཉན་པ་དེ། གནས་ཆེན་ཉེར་བཞིའི་མ་རུ་ཏ་ཡིན་ཞེས་བླ་མ་འགའ་
རེས་གསུངས།

[XXIII]

ཡང་ཨམ་འབར་སར་ནས་ལ་ཧོར་དུ་སོང་ན་དེའི་མུ་ཟེམ་ཁང་དུ་སྟོན་པ་དཀའ་བ་
སྤྱད་པའི་རྡོ་སྐུ་ངོ་མཚར་ཅན་དེ་ལ་སོགས་པ་སྔོན་གྱི་སྐུ་བརྙན་མང་དུ་བཞུགས།

Furthermore, Götsangpa dwelt there for about half a year and his precise account of the holy place has removed all uncertainty [about its identity and location]. The principal site of [Hindu] *darśan* there is the *liṅga* which resembles a head inside the Kāngra Mandir. Before one arrives in Kāngra a place called Jawala Mukhi (i.e. Jvālāmukhī) is reached. There one should have a direct encounter with the [natural] flame burning in the ground, and that was also described in the biography of Götsangpa. Taking a motorcar from Nagrota, and having passed through the town of Mandi, one arrives at Rewālsar, [which Tibetans call] Tsho Pema.[50] Also, **[22]** one reaches Kulu by motorcar after crossing the river at Mandi. That land is called Nyungti in Tibetan. As for it being Kulūta from among the twenty-four great Tantric sites, that is mentioned in many sources, and it is explained very clearly in Butön's work *bDe mchog spyi rnam* as "the cave of Nyungti behind Karsha [i.e. Lahoul]."[51] Concerning the *liṅga* which resembles the knees [of the hypostatic *vajrakāya*], it is said [by others] to be that divine representation known as Vijalīśvara which is on the peak of the eastern mountain. Yet, Butön stated that it was within a rock cave.[52] If one crosses the Rothang pass to the north of Kulu, one arrives in that Tibetan country extolled by the Drigung Kyöpa [Jigten Gompo, 1143-1217] as "Karsha Land of Ḍākinī." In that place there is [the holy mountain of] Drilburi and in the lower valley a miraculous image of Avalokiteśvara known as Ārya Triloknāth. There is a goddess known as Bhagavatī in a spot which is about half a day's walk down[stream] from the dwelling place of Ārya [Triloknāth]; that is a very rugged place which is difficult to get to, and several lamas say "It is Maruta of the twenty-four great Tantric sites."[53]

[XXII. Lahore Museum]

Also from Amritsar, if one goes to Lahore, in the museum there are housed many ancient statues, including that amazing stone image of the Teacher practising austerities [i.e. the "Fasting Buddha"].

[XXIII]

ལ་ཧོར་ནས་ར་ཝལ་པིན་ཊི་དང་དེ་ནས་གྲུ་ཟན་བཞི་ཙམ་ན་ཏག་སི་ལ་ལ་སླེབས། དེ་ནི་ཧོ་འཛོག་བྲེ་བའི་ཡུལ་སྐེ་སྟོན་རྒྱ་གར་གྱི་ [༡༣] རིག་གནས་ཀུན་གྱི་འབྱུང་ཁུངས་དང་། གྲོང་ཁྱེར་དྲུག་གི་རྒྱལ་བུ་རྣམས་ཡོན་ཏན་སློབ་ཏུ་འགྲོ་བའི་ཡུལ་ཡིན། སྨན་པ་འཚོ་བྱེད་གཞོན་ནུས་ཀྱང་དང་པོར་སྨན་འདི་ནས་བསླབ། རང་རེའི་རྒྱལ་པོ་སྲོང་བཙན་སྒམ་པོའི་དུས་ཙམ་ན་ཡུལ་འདིར་བསྟན་པ་རྒྱ་ཆེར་དར་ཞིང་ད་ལྟ་ཡང་དྷཪྨ་རཛཱིཀའི་མཆོད་རྟེན་དང་སྟོན་གྱི་དགོན་ཤུལ་མང་པོ། གྲོང་ཁྱེར་ཡོངས་རྫོགས་ཀྱི་ཤུལ་ལ་སོགས་པ་ཡོད་ཅིང་། དེ་ནས་རྙེད་པའི་སྐུ་བརྙན་རྣམས་དེ་ཀའི་མུ་ཛེམ་ན་བཞུགས་སོ།

ཏག་སི་ལ་ནས་རེ་ལི་བརྒྱུད་དེ་ནུབ་ཏུ་སོང་ན་པེས་ཤ་ཝར་ཡང་མི་རིང་ཞིང་དེ་ནི་ཐོགས་མེད་སྐུ་མཆེད་འཁྲུངས་པའི་གནས་ཡིན།

[XXIV]

ཡང་ཨ་ལ་ཧ་བ་དའམ་ལག་ནཽ་ནས་ཛྷོམ་ཛྷེ་ཕྱོགས་སུ་སོང་བས་སན་ཅི་ལ་སླེབས་དེར་ཆོས་རྒྱལ་མྱ་ངན་མེད་ཀྱི་མཆོད་རྟེན་ཆེན་པོ་ངོ་མཚར་བའི་སྒོ་བཞི་དང་ལྡན་པ་དེ་ཡོད། དེ་ནས་ཨུ་ཇེན་ལ་སླེབས། དེ་ནི་རྒྱལ་པོ་རབ་སྣང་གི་གྲོང་ཁྱེར་འཕགས་རྒྱལ་ཡིན་ཅིང་འཕགས་པ་ཀཏྱཱཡནས་བསྟན་པ་དར་བར་མཛད་པའི་གནས་ཡིན།

[XXV]

དེ་ནས་སླར་ཡང་ཛྷོམ་ཛྷེ་ཕྱོགས་སུ་སོང་བས་འཇལ་སྒོན་གྲུ་ཟན་ལ་ཐུག་ཅིང་དེ་ནས་བབས་ཏེ་མོ་ཊར་ལམ་སོང་བས་ཨ་ཇན་ཏ་ལ་སླེབས། དེ་ནི་དེང་སང་འཇིག་རྟེན་ན་གྲགས་པའི་གནས་ངོ་མཚར་ [༡༤] ཅན་ཏེ། ཕྱི་བྲག་རི་ལ་ནང་གཙུག་ལག་ཁང་ཆེ་ཆུང་སྣ་ཚོགས་པར་ཡོད་པ། ལྡེབ་རིས་ལ་སྟོན་པའི་རྣམ་ཐར་དང་སྐྱེས་རབས་ཀྱི་རི་མོ་ངོ་མཚར་བས་བརྒྱན་པ།

[XXIII. Taxila]

From Lahore one goes to Rawalpindi, and four more stations on from there one arrives at Taxila (Takṣaśilā). That is the country known as Dönjog [in Tibetan]. It was the source of all the sciences **[23]** of ancient India and the land which the princes of the six [great] cities went to for learning something useful. The physician Jīvaka Kumārabhṛta first taught medicine here as well. At about the time of our king Songtsen Gampo (d. 649), the Buddhist teachings were spread extensively in this country. Still today, there are such things as the funerary monument of Dharmarājikā, many ruins of ancient monasteries and the remains of a complete city, and the statues which were found there are housed in the museum which is right at the site.

If one continues by train to the west of there it is also not far to Peshāwar, and that was the place where the brothers Asaṅga [and Vasubandhu] were born.

[XXIV. Sāñcī and Ujjain]

By going in the direction of Bombay from Allahābād or Lucknow one arrives at Sāñcī. Here there is an amazing, large funerary monument of the Buddhist monarch Aśoka, with four gates. From there one reaches Ujjain. This was the city [known in Tibetan as] Phagyel (i.e. Ujjayinī), [capital of Avanti] under king Pradyota, and it was the site of noble Kātyāyana's efforts to spread the Buddhist teachings.

[XXV. Buddhist Cave Temples]

From there, once again, by going in the direction of Bombay one reaches the station of Jālgaon, and getting off there and proceeding by motorcar, one arrives at Ajaṇṭā. That amazing place is world famous nowadays, **[24]** and the exterior rocky hill has various large and small monastic centres within it. The painted walls are decorated with wonderful murals of the Teacher's biography and the *Jātaka* tales.

ནང་གི་ཀྭ་གདུང་ལ་སོགས་པའི་ལྷ་ཁང་དེ་དག་ཐམས་ཅད་ཀྱང་བྲག་ཧྲིལ་པོ་གཅིག་ལས་བཟོས་པ་སོགས་བློའི་ཡུལ་ལས་འདས་པའི་ངོ་མཚར་ཅན་དེ་འཛམ་བུ་གླིང་གི་སའི་སྙིང་པོ་ལྟ་བུ་ཡིན་ནོ། བྲག་ཕུག་དེར་དེང་སང་གླིང་ཆེན་དྲུག་གི་མི་ཐམས་ཅད་ཟམ་མ་ཆད་པར་འགྲོ་ཞིང་ནང་ཐཾས་ཅད་དུ་གློག་ཞུ་ཡང་སྦར་ཡོད།

ཨ་ཛན་ཏ་ནས་མོ་ཊར་ལམ་མི་རིང་བར་ཨེ་ལོ་ར་ལ་སླེབས་དེང་སང་གི་མིང་ཝ་རུ་ལ་ཟེར། དེར་ཡང་བྲག་གི་ལྷ་ཁང་སྔ་མ་དང་ཕྱོགས་མཚུངས་པ་ཡོད།

སྔར་ཨཽ་རང་ག་བྷད་ནས་རེ་ལི་ལ་ཞུ་ཊ་ཏེ་སོང་བས་མན་མ་ད་དང་དེ་ནས་ཀ་ལྱན་དེ་ནས་ལུ་ན་བ་ལ་དང་དེ་ནས་རྐང་ཐང་ལ་མི་ལི་གསུམ་ཙམ་སོང་ན་ཀར་ལི་བྱ་བའི་བྲག་ཕུག་གི་ལྷ་ཁང་ཆེན་པོ་མི་སྟོང་ཕྲག་ཙམ་ཤོང་པ་རྒྱལ་པོ་མྱ་ངན་མེད་ཀྱི་དུས་ཙམ་ན་བྱུང་བ་ཞིག་ཡོད།

[XXVI]

ཡང་པ་ཏ་ན་ནས་མུ་ཟ་ཕར་ཕུར་ལ་སོང་དེ་ནས་མོ་ཊར་ལམ་ཧྲ་ཁ་ར་བྱ་བར་མྱ་ངན་མེད་ཀྱི་རྡོ་རིང་དང་དེ་ནས་མེ་ལི་གཉིས་ [༡༥] ཙམ་ན་ཧྲ་ས་ར་བྱ་བའི་གྲོང་དང་ཉེ་བར་བཻ་ཤཱ་ལི་ཡངས་པ་ཅན་—(VESALI) གྱི་ཤུལ་ཡོད། མུ་ཟ་ཕར་པུར་ནས་རག་སོལ་ལ་འགྲོ་བའི་ལམ་དུ་ས་གོ་ལི་བྱ་བའི་གྲུ་ཟན་ནས་རེ་ལི་བརྗེས་ཏེ་ཙུང་ཟད་སོང་ན་བེ་ཏིཨ་ལ་སླེབས།

[XXVII]

འདིའི་མིང་ལ་སྔོན་བེ་དེཏ་ཟེར་ཞིང་ལུས་འཕགས་ཀྱི་ཡུལ་བྱ་བ་ཡིན། སྟོན་པ་ཡང་ཕྱོགས་འདིར་ཕེབས་ཤིང་རྒྱལ་པོ་མ་སྐྱེས་དགྲའི་ཨ་མ་ཡང་ཡུལ་འདི་ནས་ཡིན། དེར་གནས་བསྐོར་བ་ཞིག་གི་དག་སྣང་ལ་ཤར་བའི་དྲི་མེད་ཀུན་ལྡན་གྱི་ཕོ་བྲང་ཞིག་ཀྱང་ཡོད། དེ་ནས་རག་སོལ་ལ་འགྲོ་ཞིང་དེ་བལ་ཡུལ་གྱི་ས་མཚམས་ཡིན།

The pillars, beams and so on, inside of all those temples are also fashioned out of solid rock—the marvel of such things is beyond the imagination, they are like the Southern Continent's quintessential spot! Nowadays, all peoples of the six continents come continually to the rock caves, and the whole interior has become illuminated with electric lighting as well.

It is not far by motorcar from Ajaṇṭā to reach Ellorā. Today it has the name Warul. In that place as well there are rock temples similar to the aforementioned ones.

Again, if one takes the train from Aurangabad to Manmād, and then on to Kalyān and Lonavale, and then from there going about three miles on foot, there is a large rock cave temple called Kārli with room for about one thousand people, dating from about the time of the Buddhist monarch Aśoka.

[XXVI. Vaiśālī]

One goes to Muzaffarpur from Patna as well. From there one goes by motorcar to the Aśokan stone pillar in the place called Bhakhra, and then after about two miles **[25]** there are the ruins of Vaiśālī, Yangpachen [in Tibetan]—(VESALI) near a town called Bhasara. On the line which goes to Raxaul from Muzaffarpur, one changes trains at the station called Sagauli, and then going on just a little one arrives in Bettiah.

[XXVII. Videha and Kathmandu Valley]

The ancient name of this place [i.e. Bettiah] was Videha, and it is known as the country of Lüphag [in Tibetan]. The Teacher also came to this region, and the mother of king Ajātaśatru was from this country as well. There was also a palace of Drimé Kunden which appeared in the pure vision of a pilgrim in that place.[54] One proceeds to Raxaul from there and that is the frontier of Nepal.

རག་སོལ་ནས་རེལ་ཆུང་དང་མོ་ཊར་བརྒྱུད་ནས་ལ་རྩ་བར་དང་། དེ་ནས་རྐང་འགྲོས་ཀྱིས་ཉིན་གཉིས་ལ་བལ་ཡུལ་མཐིལ་དུ་སླེབས། དེར་རྟེན་གྱི་གཙོ་བོ་*svayambhū* རང་བྱུང་མཆོད་རྟེན་ཤིང་ཀུན་དང་། བྱ་རུང་ཁ་ཤོར། སྟག་མོ་ལུས་སྦྱིན་སོགས་གནས་རྟེན་ཤིན་ཏུ་མང་པོ་དང་། གཞན་ཡང་དམ་པ་འགའ་ཞིག་གིས་ཡུལ་འདི་ལི་ཡུལ་དུ་ངོས་བཟུང་བ་ལ་བརྟེན། གླང་རུ་ལུང་བསྟན་ནས་གསུངས་པའི་གནས་རྣམས་ཀྱང་ཡུལ་འདིར་མཇལ་རྒྱུ་ཡོད་དོ། ཕྱོགས་འདིར་བོད་རིགས་དང་། བལ་པོ་བོད་སྐད་ལ་བྱང་བ་མང་དུ་ཡོད་ཅིང་། གནས་རྣམས་རྩད་གཅོད་བདེ་བས་འདིར་ཞིབ་ཏུ་མ་བྲིས། [༡༨]

[XXVIII]

ཡང་གྷ་ཡ་ནས་ཀ་ལི་ཀ་ཏར་འགྲོ་བའི་ལམ་དུ་སུལ་ཏན་གན་ཛེ་བྱ་བའི་གྲུ་ཟན་ལ་སླེབས། དེར་གྲོང་དང་ཉེ་བའི་གདྷའི་ཆུ་དཀྱིལ་ན་བྲག་རི་ལྷ་ཁང་ཅན་ཞིག་ཡོད་པའི་ཆུར་ངོས་ཀྱི་ཆུ་འགྲམ་བྲག་རི་ཆུང་དུ་ཞིག་ཡོད་ས་དེ་པི་ཀྲམ་ལ་ཤི་ལའི་དགོན་ཤུལ་ཡིན་ཀྱང་ས་མ་བརྐོས་པས་ས་མིག་འདི་ཡིན་ན་དུང་མི་ཤེས། དེ་ནས་སོང་པས་ཧྥང་གལ་པུར་དུ་སླེབས་ཅིང་དེ་ནི་སྟོན་གྱི་ཛཧྣལའི་རྒྱལ་ཁབ་ཏེ་སློབ་དཔོན་ཞི་བ་འཚོ་དང་ཇོ་བོ་རྗེ་འཁྲུངས་པའི་གནས་ཡིན་ཅིང་ཡུལ་ཙམྤ་ཡང་དེ་ཡིན། ཟ་ཧོར་རམ་ས་ཧོ་ར་ཡང་དེ་དང་ཉེ་བ་ན་སྟོན་གྱི་ཕོ་བྲང་གི་ཤུལ་སོགས་ཡོད་ཟེར།

[XXIX]

ཀ་ལི་ཀ་ཏ་ནས་རེལ་དང་འཛའ་ཅི་ལས་ཤར་ཕྱོགས་སུ་ཆེར་མི་རིང་བ་ན་ཅི་ཊ་གོང་ཡོད།

Having continued by small[-gauge] rail line and motorcar from Raxaul as far as the foot of the pass, after two days travel on foot from there one reaches the centre of Nepal [i.e. Kathmandu Valley]. In that region, there are very many holy places and sacred representations, including the principal sacred representation, the Svayambhū[nāth] self-arisen funerary monument which [Tibetans call Phagpa] Shingkun, the [funerary monument of] Jarung Khashor (i.e. Bodhnāth), and Tagmo Lüchin (i.e. Namobuddha). Furthermore, in keeping with the acknowledgment of this country as Liyül (i.e. Khotan) by some holy persons, the places which are mentioned in the *Gośṛṅgavyākaraṇa*[*-sūtra*] also should be directly encountered in this country.[55] In this region there are many Tibetans, and Nepalese who have learned the Tibetan language, and because it is easy to inquire after its holy places I will not write in detail here **[26]**.

[XXVIII. Vikramaśilā and Sahor]

On the rail line which goes from Gayā to Calcutta again, one reaches the station called Sultanganj. Close to the town, the river bank on the near side, where there is a rocky outcrop with a temple in the middle of the river Gangā, has a small rock hill. That spot is the ruined monastery of Vikramaśilā. However, because the area has not been excavated it is still unknown whether this is the exact spot. By going on from there one arrives in Bhagalpur, and that was the royal court of Bengal in the past and the birth place of the teacher Śāntarakṣita and the Lord Atiśa (982?-1054?). That was also the country of Campā. Zahor, or Sahor [as the Indians pronounce it], was also close by to it, and it is said there are such things as the ruins of its former palace.[56]

[XXIX. Chittagong]

Not too far east from Calcutta by train and ship[57] there is Chittagong.

དེར་མ་ཏྲ་སྨུ་ནིའི་གཙུག་ལག་ཁང་སོགས་དང་དགེ་འདུན་གྱི་སྡེ་མང་དུ་བཞུགས། ཡུལ་དེར་ནི་སྔོན་ནས་ད་ལྟའི་བར་བསྟན་པ་མ་ཉམས་པར་བཞུགས་ཤིང་། པཎྜིཏ་ནགས་ཀྱི་རིན་ཆེན་བྱོན་ས་ཡང་འདི་ཡིན་པར་སེམས།

[XXX]

ཡང་པཏྣ་ཧྲི་པུར་ནས་སློ་ཏ་ཏ་བར་རེལ་ལེ་དང་དེ་ནས་མེ་ལེ་བཅུ་བདུན་སོང་པ་ན་ཤར་རྩ་མཆོག་གྲོང་(མ་ཏྲ་སྨུ་ནི་)ཡོད། དེ་ནི་གནས་ཆེན་ཉེར་བཞིའི་ཡ་གྱལ་གྱི་ཀ་མ་རུ་པ་ཡིན་འདུག་ཅིང་། སྔོན་མདོ་སྔགས་གཉིས་ཀའི་བསྟན་པ་ཤིན་ཏུ་དར་བའི་གནས་ཡིན། [༢༧]

[XXXI]

ཡང་ཀ་ལི་ཀ་ཏ་ནས་མེ་ཧྲི་ར་ས་ལ་འགྲོ་བའི་རེལ་ལེ་ལ་ཞུགས་ཏེ་ཕྱིན་པས་ཐོག་མར་ཨོ་རི་ས་ལ་སླེབས། ཡུལ་དེ་ནི་ཨོ་ཏི་བི་ཤའམ་ཀ་ལིངྐའི་ཡུལ་དེ་སྔོན་གསང་སྔགས་དར་བའི་གནས་ཡིན་ཅིང་ད་དུང་ཡང་དེར་ནང་པའི་སྔགས་ཉམས་སུ་ལེན་པ་ཡོད་ཅེས་ཐེར། ཡུལ་དེར་རྒྱ་མཚོའི་འགྲམ་དང་ཉེ་བ་ན་(པུ་རི་)ཛ་གད་ན་ཐ་བྲ་བའི་ཁྲབ་འཇུག་གི་ལྷ་ཁང་ངོ་མཚར་ཅན་དེ་ཡོད།

[XXXII]

ཨོ་རི་ས་ནས་སྟར་གྱི་རེལ་ལམ་བརྒྱུད་དེ་ལྷོ་ཕྱོགས་སུ་སོང་[༡༨] བ་ལས་ཆུ་བོ་གྲིཥྞ་བཏལ། ཏེཟ་བ་དའི་གྲུ་ཟན་ནས་རེལ་ལི་བརྗེས་ཏེ་ཏྲུན་ཏུར་ལ་འགྲོ། དེ་ནས་མོ་ཏར་ལས་ཤྲི་ཧྲ་ན་ཀྭ་ཏ་ལ་སླེབས་ཅིང་དེ་འབྲས་སྤུངས་མཆོད་རྟེན་གྱི་གནས་ཤུལ་འཁྲུལ་མེད་དེ་ཡིན། དེ་ནས་མེ་ལི་བཅོ་ལྔ་ཙམ་ཆུ་འགྲམ་ཕྱོགས་སུ་སོང་བས་ན་གར་ཀོན་ཏ་བྲ་བ་ཀླུ་ཕྱོགས་དཔལ་གྱི་རི་ཀླུ་སྒྲུབ་ཡབ་སྲས་བཞུགས་ས་དེར་སླེབས། དེར་མཛལ་ཀྱུ་ཡང་མང་པོ་ཡོད།།

---

༡༨) *Orig.* སོང་སོང་།

In that place many communities of monks reside in monastic centres such as the Mahāmuni. In that land, from former times up until the present day, the Buddhist teachings have remained intact and I consider this to also be the place from which the paṇḍita Vanaratna (b.1348) came.[58]

[XXX. Kāmarūpa]

One goes by rail from Parbatipur as far as Gauhāti, and then seventeen miles on, there is the eastern Kuśinagarī (Mahāmuni). That is Kāmarūpa which is one of the twenty-four great Tantric sites, and it is an area where the Buddhist teachings of both *sūtra* and *mantra* where widely spread in the past **[27]**.

[XXXI. Orissa]

From Calcutta again, one stays on the train which goes to Madras, and one arrives at first in Orissa. That land was Oḍiviśa or the country of Kaliṅga and a place where the Secret Mantra was spread, and it is said "Buddhist Mantra[yāna] can still be ascertained there." In that region, close to the shore of the ocean, there is that wonderful temple of Viṣṇu known as Purī Jagannāth.

[XXXII. Dhānyakaṭaka and Śrī Parvata]

Going south from Orissa on the same rail line as before, as one proceeds one crosses over the river Kṛṣṇā. One changes trains at the station of Vijayawāda, and travels to Guntur. From there by motorcar one reaches Śrī Dhanakoṭa, and that is indisputably the ruins of the holy place of the Dhānyakaṭaka funerary monument.[59] By going along the river bank about fifteen miles from there one arrives at that site where Nāgārjuna and his disciple [Āryadeva] dwelt called Nāgār[juni]koṇḍa, the southern Śrī Parvata. In that place there is still much that could be visited.

[XXXIII]

དེ་ནས་ཀུན་དར་ནས་སྨར་རེ་ལ་ལི་ཞུགས་ཏེ་ཊེ་ན་ལི་དང་དེ་ནས་མེ་དྷི་ར་ས་བརྒྱུད་དེ་ར་མེ་ཤྭར་བར་འགྲོ ར་མེ་ཤྭར་ཡང་གནས་ཆེན་ཉེར་བཞིའི་ནང་གི་གཅིག་ཡིན་ཅིང་། དེ་ནས་མི་གྲུ་ལས་མཚོ་ལ་ཐུང་ཟད་སོང་པས་སིནྷ་ལའི་གླིང་དུ་སླེབས། [༣༦]

དེར་རྩ་བའི་སྡེ་བ་གནས་བརྟན་པ་ལས་གྱེས་པའི་དགེ་འདུན་གྲངས་མེད་པ་བཞུགས་ཤིང་བསྟན་པ་རྒྱ་ཆེར་དར། འཇིགས་མེད་རི་དང་། རྒྱལ་བྱེད་ཚལ། གཙུག་ལག་ཁང་ཆེན་པོ་གསུམ་ཀའི་རྩ་བའི་གནས་གཞི་དག་ཀྱང་གླིང་འདིར་ཡོད། སྟོན་པ་འདས་ནས་ལོ་སུམ་བརྒྱ་ཙམ་ན་ཧྨཱ་ཨཤྭོ་ཀའི་སྲས་གནས་བརྟན་དབང་ཆེན་སྡེ་དང་། དེའི་སྲིང་མོ་འཕགས་མ་དགེ་འདུན་རྩ་ལག་མ་གཉིས་ཀས་གནས་འདིར་བསྟན་པ་ཐོག་མར་སྤེལ་ཞིང་། དེ་ནས་བཟུང་བཙུན་པ་སངས་རྒྱས་དབྱངས་དང་། དགྲ་བཅོམ་མལླི་ཡ་དེ་བ། གནས་བརྟན་སྐྱབས་མཛད་ལ་སོགས་པའི་ཉན་ཐོས་ཆེན་པོ་རྣམས་དང་། ཆོས་ཀྱི་རྒྱལ་པོ་སྐར་རྒྱལ་དང་། འཇིགས་མེད་དང་། དུ་ཏ་ག་མི་ན་དང་། པར་ཀྲམ་བཱ་ཧུ་ (ཟླ་གནོན་དཔུང་བ་) སོགས་བསྟན་པའི་སྦྱིན་བདག་ཆེན་པོ་རྣམས་ཀྱི་བཀའ་དྲིན་ལ་བརྟེན། རྒྱལ་བའི་བསྟན་པ་ལོ་ཉིས་སྟོང་ལྷག་གི་ཡུན་ལ་གནས་ཤིང་། ནང་པའི་རྒྱལ་ཁམས་ཀུན་ལས་རྙིང་ཤོས་ལྟ་བུ་ཡིན། ནང་གསེས་ཀྱི་མཁན་བརྒྱུད་མི་འདྲ་བའི་སྡེ་པ་གསུམ་བཞུགས། གནས་བརྟན་པའི་ལུང་ལ་སྡེ་སྣོད་གསུམ་ལས། འདུལ་བ་ལ་ཕམ་པ་ལ་སོགས་པའི་སྡེ་ཚན་བདུན། མདོ་སྡེ་ལ་ལུང་རིང་པོ་དང་། བར་མ་ལ་སོགས་པ་ཚན་ལྔ་། མངོན་པ་ལ་ཁམས་ཀྱི་གཏམ་ལ་སོགས་པ་བདུན། དེ་དག་རེ་རེ་ལ་ཡང་མདོ་ཕྲན་དུ་མ་དང་། དེ་དག་གི་དགོངས་འགྲེལ་སངས་རྒྱས་དབྱངས་སོགས་ཀྱིས་མཛད་པ་བཅས་རྒྱ་ཆེར་ཡོད་དོ། རྟེན་གྱི་གཙོ་བོར་གྱུར་པ་ནི་ཀན་ཌི་ན་ [༣༧] ཀ་ལིངྒའི་རྒྱལ་པོའི་གདུང་སྐལ་སྟོན་པའི་ཚེམས་མཆེ་བ་དང་། ཨ་ནུ་ར་ཋ་པུ་ར་ན་སྒྲ་ངན་མེད་ཀྱིས་སྐྲིས་སུ་གནང་བའི་བྱང་ཆུབ་ཤིང་། རི་བོ་ཤྲཱི་པ་དའི་རྩེར་སྟོན་པའི་ཞབས་རྗེས་བཅས་ཡོད།

[XXXIII. Ceylon]

Taking the train from there once again to Guntur, and passing through Tenali and then Madras, one travels as far as Rāmeśvara. Rāmeśvara is one of the twenty-four great Tantric sites as well. With a short trip across the straits from there by steamer one arrives in Ceylon (see figure 5) **[28]**.

In that place dwell countless monks who are a division of the original Theravāda [order], and the Buddhist teachings are well developed. There were on this island also the three original [sectarian] seats of Abhayagiri, Jetavana and Mahāvihāra. About three hundred years after the Teacher passed away both Dharmāśoka's son, the Thera Mahinda, and his sister, the noble Saṃghamittā, began propagating the Buddhist teachings in this place. And, they took hold after that, supported by the grace of the great Śrāvakas, including the venerable Buddhaghosa (5th cent.), the Arahant Malaya-Mahādeva and the Thera Saraṇaṅkara, and the great patrons, including the Buddhist kings Phussa, Abhaya, Duṭṭhagāmaṇi (c. 1st cent. B.C.E.) and Parākramabāhu (1153-1186). The Buddha's teachings persevered here for a period of over two thousand years, and it is evidently the oldest of all [surviving] Buddhist kingdoms. Three different schools of reciprocal abbatial lineages still exist. According to the *Tripiṭaka* in the Theravāda transmission, the *Vinaya* has seven sections including the *pārājika*, in the *Sūtra* section there are five divisions, the long transmission, the middle and so on, and in the *Abhidharma* there are seven, including the discourse on the elements. There are also numerous minor *sūtra*-s within each of them, and the commentaries on these, including those made by Buddhaghosa, are extensive. Concerning what have become [Ceylon's] principal sacred representations **[29]**, there is the Teacher's canine tooth—the relic portion of the king of Kaliṅga—in Kandy, together with the Bodhi Tree at Anurādhapura which was given as a gift by Aśoka, and the Teacher's footprint on the peak of the Śrīpādaparvata (i.e. Adam's Peak).

ས་ག་ཟླ་བའི་ཉའི་ཉིན་མོ་འཛིག་རྟེན་ན་དཔེ་མེད་པའི་སངས་རྒྱས་པའི་དུས་སྟོན་ཆེན་པོ་བྱེད་དོ།

སིདྡྷ་ལ་ཡི་གནས་བརྟན་སྡེ་པ་དང་།
གངས་རིའི་ལྗོངས་ཀྱི་ཡོད་པར་སྨྲ་བ་གཉིས།
སྟོན་པ་གཅིག་གིས་བསྐྱངས་པའི་སློབ་མ་སྟེ།
བཅོ་བརྒྱད་སྡེ་བ་ནུབ་པའི་ལྷག་མ་ཉིད། ཅེས་ཀྱང་སྨྲས་སོ།

[XXXIV]

ཀ་ལི་ཀ་ཏ་ནས་སྐོར་བཅོ་ལྔ་ཙམ་ལ་འཇའ་ཅི་ནས་ཕྱིན་པས་ཧྲར་མ་རན་ཀུན་དུ་སླེབས། དེར་ཡང་དགེ་སློང་ཁྲི་ཁྲག་དུ་མ་བཞུ་ཞིང་། ཡོངས་སུ་གྲགས་པའི་མཆོད་རྟེན་ཆེན་པོ་གསེར་གྱི་པ་གོ་ཌ་དེ་ནི་སྟོན་པའི་ཐོག་མར་བཀྲ་ཤིས་ཀྱི་ཚིགས་བཅད་གསུང་ཡུལ་གྱི་ཚོང་པ་ག་གོན་དང་བཟང་པོ་གཉིས་ཧྲར་མ་ནས་ཡིན་པས་དེ་གཉིས་ཀྱིས་སྟོན་པའི་དབུ་སྐྲ་དང་སེན་མོ་བླངས་ཏེ་མཆོད་རྟེན་བརྩིགས་པ་ཡིན་ཅེས་ཁོང་དག་ཟེར།

[XXXV]

རན་གུན་ནས་སིདྡྷ་པུར་བར་སྐོར་ཉི་ཤུ་ཙམ་རེ་ལ་གླ་དང་དེ་ནས་འཇའ་ཅི་ལས་སྐོར་བཙུ་ཙམ་ན་སུམ་ཏར་ལ་སླེབས། དེ་ནི་གསེར་གླིང་སྟེ་བསྟན་པ་ནི་མེད། [༡༠]

[XXXVI]

གསེར་གླིང་གི་ཤར་ལྷོ་ཕྱོགས་སུ་འཇའ་བའམ་འབྲུའི་གླིང་ཡོད། ཞི་བ་སྲས་པའི་སྐབས་གླིང་འདིར་ད་དུང་ཡང་བསྟན་པ་གནས་ཚུལ་བཤད། སིདྡྷ་པུར་ནས་འཇའ་ཅི་ལས་སྐོར་བཞི་བཙུ་ཙམ་གྱིས་སླེབས། དེར་བསྟན་པ་ནི་མེད།

On the full moon day of the fourth month a great Buddhist festival which is unique throughout the world is staged.[60]

It is also said:

> Both the Theravāda of Ceylon and,
> The Sarvāstivādins of Tibet,
> Are students who were looked after by one and the same teacher,
> And of the eighteen [original Buddhist] orders, they are the only active remainder.[61]

[XXXIV. Burma]

One reaches Rangoon in Burma having gone by ship from Calcutta for about 15 *rupees*. In that place also there dwell many tens of thousands of fully ordained monks. Concerning the great funerary monument here which is very famous, that *pagoda* of gold [i.e. Shwedagon], they say that, "Both the provincial merchants Trapuṣa and Bhallika to whom the Teacher first uttered auspicious verses were from Burma, and therefore those two obtained the Teacher's head hair and fingernails and the [first] funerary monument was built."[62]

[XXXV. Sumatra]

From Rangoon as far as Singapore the train fare is about 20 *rupees*, and from there by ship for about 10 *rupees* one reaches Sumatra. That place is Suvarṇadvīpa and the Buddhist teachings do not exist there **[30]**.

[XXXVI. Java]

Java or Dhānyadvīpa is to the southeast of Suvarṇadvīpa. On this island during the time of Śāntigupta (16th cent.) narrations of the Buddhist teachings were still being preached.[63] From Singapore one gets there by ship for about 40 *rupees*. The Buddhist teachings do not exist there [nowadays].

ཛྙ་རོ་ཛྙ་དུ་ར་བྱ་བའི་སྟོན་གྱི་མཆོད་རྟེན་རི་ཆེན་པོ་ལྟ་བུ། བང་རིམ་གྲུ་བཞི་པ་ལྔ་། ཀླུམ་པོ་དྲུག་ཀླུམ་པོ་འོག་མར་མཆོད་རྟེན་ཆུང་ངུ་སོ་གཉིས། དེའི་སྟེང་མར་ཉེར་བཞི། དེའི་སྟེང་མར་བཅུ་དྲུག དབུས་སུ་མཆོད་རྟེན་ཆེན་པོ་གཅིག་བཅས་ངོ་མཚར་བའི་རྨི་ལམ་གཟུགས་སུ་གྲུབ་པ་འདྲ་བ་ཞིག་ཡོད་པ་དེ་གནས་བསྐོར་བ་ཞིག་གིས་གསར་དུ་མཐོང་ན་འབྲས་སྤུངས་མཆོད་རྟེན་དུ་བྱེད་རྒྱུར་འདུག་ཅིང་། མན་ལུང་གུ་རུའི་དགོངས་ཚོད་ཀྱང་དེ་ཡིན་རྒྱུར་འདུག་གོ །

[XXXVII]

ཛྙར་མའི་ཤར་རྒྱ་ནག་ཏུ་ཆུ་ཐོག་བརྒྱུད་ནས་འགྲོ་བའི་ལམ་དུ་སི་ཡམ་གྱི་ཡུལ་ཡོད་ཅིང་། དེར་བསྟན་པ་ཤིན་ཏུ་དར། དགོན་གནས་ཆེ་ཆུང་སྡོམ་པ་རང་ཡང་ཚིག་ཁྲི་དྲུག་སྟོང་ལྷག་ཙམ་དང་། རྒྱལ་ས་འབན་ཀོག་ཏུ་ཕར་ཀོའོ་བྱ་བའི་གཙུག་ལག་ཁང་ན་ལྷའི་དབང་པོས་བཟོས་པར་གྲགས་པའི་མརྐད་ལས་གྲུབ་པའི་སྟོན་པའི་སྐང་བརྙན་འཛམ་གླིང་གི་ནོར་གྱི་རིན་ཐང་ཅན་དུ་གྲགས་པ་བཅས་བཞུགས། [༣༧]

[XXXVIII]

དེ་ལྟར་ན་ཉན་ཐོས་ཀྱི་སྡེ་སྣོད་གཙོ་བོར་དར་བའི་ཡུལ་ནི་ཛྙར་མ། སི་ཡམ། སེངྒ་ལ་གསུམ་པོ་འདི་ཡིན་ལུགས། སི་ཡམ་གྱི་ཤར་ཕྱོགས་ཨིན་ཌོ་ཅི་ནའི་ཡུལ་དུ་ཡང་བསྟན་པ་དར་ཞིང་དགེ་སློང་མང་དུ་བཞུགས། རྒྱ་སྐད་དུ་ཡུལ་འདི་ལ་ཀ་སྦོ་ཛ་ཞེས་གྲགས། རྒྱ་ནག་སྟོང་ཁྲུན་ཞེས་ཟེར་བ་ཡང་ཡུལ་འདིའི་རྒྱལ་ས་རྙིང་པའི་མིང་ཡིན་ཞིང་། སྔར་ཟ་ཧོར་དང་འདི་གཉིས་ཕན་ཚུན་འབྲེལ་ཆེ་བའི་ལོ་རྒྱུས་མང་ངོ་།

There is an ancient funerary monument called Barabuḍur resembling a large hill, with a five-tiered rectangular base, six[64] circular [terraces], thirty-two smaller funerary monuments on the lower circular [terrace], twenty-four on the one above that, sixteen on the one above that and one large funerary monument in the centre. It is just like a marvelous dream realized in solid form. If that is seen by a pilgrim for the first time, it could be taken for the funerary monument of Dhānyakaṭaka.[65] Manlung Guru (b.1239) also conjectured that it could be so.

[XXXVII. Siam]

The county of Siam is east of Burma on the route which passes over a part of the river going to China, and the Buddhist teachings are widely spread in that place. Even the total of large and small monastic sites exceeds sixteen thousand, and in the monastic centre (i.e. *wat*) called Phra Keo, in the capital Bangkok, there resides an image of the Teacher made out of emeralds which is famous as having been crafted by Indra and possessing reportedly the world's most valuable gemstones **[31]**.

[XXXVIII. Cambodia and Indo-China]

In accord with that [description above], the lands in which the Theravādan *Tripiṭaka* is principally spread are these three: Burma, Siam and Ceylon. Also in the region of Indo-China, to the east of Siam, the Buddhist teachings are spread and fully ordained monks dwell there. In Sanskrit this land is renowned as Kamboja.[66] In China the name of the old capital of this land was also called Tongking,[67] and there are many historical narratives about the high degree of mutual contacts between both it and Zahor in the past.

[XXXIX]

དེ་ལྟར་གོང་དུ་ཁ་ཆེན་བཅད་དེ་ངོས་བཟུང་བའི་གནས་དེ་དག་ནི་སྔོན་གྱི་རབས་ལ་དཔྱད་པ་རྫོགས་པའི་མཁས་པ་རྣམས་ལ་དྲི་གཏུག་དང་བོད་ཀྱི་ལོ་རྒྱུས་རྙིང་པ་འབྲེལ་མེད་རྣམས་དང་ཡང་ཞིབ་ཏུ་བསྡྲི་ཊ་ཏེ་མཚན་མཚོན་ངོ་འཕྲོད་ནས་བྲིས་པ་ཡིན་གྱི། ཡིན་ནམ་སྙམ་པ་ལ་ཡིན་ནོ་ཞེས་ཁ་ཐད་བྱས་པ་ཙུང་ཟད་ཀྱང་མེད་པས་ཐེ་ཚོམ་ཕྲ་མོ་ཙམ་ཡང་མི་དགོས་སོ།

གཞན་གནས་བསྐོར་བ་རེས་གནས་རྒྱུས་མེད་དུ་སླེབས་ནས་ལྷ་ཁང་དོ་མཚར་ཅན་རེ་མཐོང་བ་ན། རྒྱུ་མཚན་ཅི་ཡང་མེད་པར་འདི་སངས་རྒྱས་ཀྱི་གནས་ག་གེ་མོ་དང་ཆེ་གེ་མོ་ཡིན་ནོ་ཞེས་ངེས་བཟུང་། གཏམ་དེ་གཅིག་གིས་གཅིག་ལ་བསྒྲགས་[༢༠] ཏེ་གྲགས་བྱུང་བའི་གནས་ཀྱང་ལོ་རེ་བཞིན་མང་དུ་འགྲོ་བར་འདུག་པས། རྣམ་དབྱེ་ལེགས་པར་ [༡༢] ཕྱེད་དགོས་ཏེ། དཔེར་ན་ཆོས་འཁོར་བསྐོར་བའི་གནས་ལྷ་བུ་ཞིག་ལ་མཚོན་ན། དང་པོ་བོད་སྐད་དུ་གནས་དེའི་མིང་ལ་གང་ཟེར་ཤེས་དགོས། དེ་ལ་དྲང་སྲོང་ལྷུང་བ་ཟེར། དེ་ནས་བོད་ཚིག་དེ་དང་པོ་རྒྱ་སྐད་གང་ལས་བསྒྱུར་བ་ཤེས་དགོས། དེ་ལ་རི་ཥི་པ་ཏ་ན་ཟེར། དེ་ནས་རི་ཥི་པ་ཏ་ན་ལ་དེང་སང་གང་ཟེར་དྲིས་པས་ས་ར་ན་ཐ་ཟེར་བ་སོགས་རིམ་པར་སྦྱར་ནས་མཐར་ཉེ་འཁོར་གྱི་གྲོང་ཁྱེར་དང་མཐའ་ན་ཨ་སི་དང་ཝ་ར་ཎའི་ཆུ་ཀླུན་ཆད་ཀྱང་ངོ་འཕྲོད་ནས་གནས་གཅིག་ངོས་འཛིན་དགོས་པ་ཡིན་གྱི། དང་པོ་ཐམ་ཐོམ་ལ་སླྲས། རྗེས་སུ་དད་པ་ཡོད་ན་གང་ཡང་རུང་ཞེས་ཨུ་ཚུགས་བྱས་ཏེ། གནས་དངོས་མ་དང་བརྫུན་མ་འདི་ཡིན་སྙོན་རྒྱུ་མེད་པ་དེ་འདྲ་མི་གནང་བར་གསོལ་བ་ལན་བརྒྱར་འདེབས་པ་ལགས།། [༡༡]

༢༠) *Orig.* སྒྲགས།

[XXXIX. Identification and Authenticity]

Concerning those acknowledged holy places determined in accord with the above [exposition], I have put questions to scholars who exhaustively investigated their ancient narratives and matched them exactly with indisputably old Tibetan histories as well, and I wrote having identified the characteristics they exhibit. Since I have not even made the slightest boast that "I think it might be, therefore it is!", one need not have even a shred of doubt.

When some other pilgrims arrive at an unknown site and see a marvelous temple, without any evidence whatsoever they take it to be authentic, proclaiming "This is such-and-such and so-and-so holy place of the Buddha." They call out the news to one another, and so the places which are becoming famous are even increasing annually. Therefore, **[32]** distinguishing features ought to be properly analyzed. For example, if we illustrate this with regard to the place where the wheel of the Buddhist doctrine was [first] turned: Initially, it is necessary to know what the name of that place is in Tibetan. It is Drangsong Lungwa. Then it is necessary to know what earlier Sanskrit that Tibetan word was translated from. It was Ṛṣipatana. Then there is the question of what Ṛṣipatana is called nowadays: it is called Sārnāth. After gradually compiling such [evidence], and finally identifying the city which is in the vicinity [i.e. Vārāṇasī] and that it is within the confines of the Asī and Varaṇā rivers as well, then one holy place should be recognized. But, at first talk is muddled. Following that, if [people] have faith they insist on whatever was said, and are unable to distinguish a true holy place and a false one. I request you a hundred times please not to accept that sort of thing! **[33]**.

[IL]

།གནས་ཆེན་གཞན་འགའ་ཞིག་གི་ཐོ།

འདིར་བརྒྱུད་སྟེ་ནས་གསུངས་པའི་གནས་ཆེན་ཉེར་བཞི་པོ་རྣམས་ནི་ཕྱི་ནང་ཐུན་མོང་གི་གནས་ཡིན་སྐབས། དེ་དག་གི་སྔགས་སྐད་ཀྱི་མིང་རྣམས་བཏ་འཕྲོད་ན། ཕལ་ཆེར་ཞིག་ཇོ་ཀི་རྣམས་ཀྱིས་ཀྱང་ཤེས། ཀཱ་མ་རཱུ་པ་= *kāmarūpa* ཀུ་ལུ་ཏ་= *kulu* གོ་ད་ཝ་རི་= *godāvarī-nisak* ཨོ་ཏེ་= *orisa* ཨོ་ཏེ་བི་ཤ་དང་དོན་གཅིག རཱ་མེ་ཤྭར་=*rāmeśvara* ལམྦྷག་= *lambhaga* སྐེ་འདི་སིན་དྷུའི་ཡུལ་ཆ་སྐེ། ཀཱཏྱཡནའི་ལོ་རྒྱུས་སུ་འབྱུང་བ་པ་ཞེས་བསྒྱུར་བ་དེ་དང་གཅིག སིན་དྷུ་=*sindhu* ནགར་=*śrīnagara* ཁ་ཆེའི་གྲོང་ཡིན། མ་ལ་ཝ་= *mālavar* རཥྚ་= *mahārasṭa* གོང་དུ་བཤད་པའི་གྲོང་ཁྱེར་པ་ཏ་ལི་པུ་ཏྲ་ནི་པུཥྤི་རཱ་མ་ཡིན་ཞེས། བུ་སྟོན་དང་མཁས་གྲུབ་སོགས་ཀྱིས་གསུངས།

[ILI]

པེས་ཤ་ཝར་ནས་མ་ལ་གཎ་དུ་འགྲོ། དེ་ནས་རྐང་འགྲོས་ཀྱིས་སྭཏ་བྱ་བའི་ལུང་པར་སླེབས་ཤིང་དེ་ཨོ་རྒྱན་གྱི་གནས་ལྟེ་བ་དེ་ཡིན། སྭཏ་བྱ་བ་ཁ་ནས་བརྗོད་ཚེ་ས་བད་ཅེས་དྲི་དགོས་ཤིང་། བཏ་མ་འཕྲོད་ན་རྒྱ་ཡིག *svāt* དབྱིན་ཡིག *Swat*[༧༧]*-Valley* འདི་བསྟན་ན་ཤེས། ཡུལ་དེར་ཨོ་ཊེ་གྲམ་ *odegram* བྱ་བ་ཡོད་ཅིང་དེ་རྫུ་མ་ཐ་ལའི་གྲོང་ཡིན།

དེ་ཡང་ཨོ་རྒྱན་གྱི་ཡུལ་འདི་ནི་ཤིན་ཏུ་ [༡༩] གྲགས་ཆེ་བའི་རྒྱུ་མཚན་གྱིས། ངོ་མཚར་བའི་གཏམ་བརྒྱུད་སྣ་ཚོགས་ཀྱིས་གཡོགས་ཏེ། ཐོས་རྒྱ་ཆུང་ཞིང་ཧར་ལ་དགའ་བའི་མི་མང་པོ་ཞིག་གིས་ནི། ངེད་ཀྱིས་སྨྲས་པ་འདི་ལ་ཡིད་ཆེས་པར་ཤིན་ཏུ་དཀའ་མོད་ཀྱི། ཆེས་སྔ་མོའི་དུས་ན་ཕྱོགས་འདིར་དངོས་སུ་བྱོན་ཞིང་ལམ་ཡིག་བྲིས་པ། ཐང་གི་གོང་མའི་ཕོ་ཉ་ཧྱུང་ཡུན་དང་། ནུབ་ཕྱོགས་ཀྱི་རྒྱལ་པོ་ཨེ་ལེག་སན་ཌར་དང་།

༧༧) *Orig.* Swal (in Roman script)

[IL.] A List of Some Other Great Tantric Sites

In this [section], concerning the twenty-four great Tantric sites which are mentioned in the Tantras, they are places which are common to non-Buddhists and Buddhists. If their Sanskrit names are given in written form most yogis will also recognize them: Kā-ma-rū-pa=*Kāmarūpa*; Ku-lū-ta=*Kulu*; Go-da-wa-ri=*Godāvarī-Nisak*; O-ṭi=*Orisa*, which stands for Oḍiviśa; Rāmeśwara=*Rāmeśvara*; Lambaka=*Lambhaga,* and this is part of the country of Sindhu, and it is the same as that translated as Changwapa [in Tibetan] in the historical narrative of Kātyāyana; Sin-dhu=*Sindhu*; Nagara=*Śrīnagara*, it is the town of Kashmir; Ma-la-wa=*Mālavar*; Raṣṭa=*Mahāraṣṭa*; and concerning the city of Pāṭaliputra which was discussed above, the likes of Butön and Khedrup[je] (1385-1438) have stated, "It is Pullīrama[laya]."

[ILI. Uḍḍiyāna]

From Peshāwar one goes to Malakand. By proceeding on foot from there one arrives in the valley called Swāt, and that is the centre of the holy place of Uḍḍiyāna. When making enquiries about Swāt [nowadays] it is necessary to ask for "Swad" and, if one cannot convey that, when one shows this: *Swat-Valley* in written English or *Svāt* in written Hindi, it will be understood. That land is known as Uḍe-grām, and the town of Dhūmatāla is there.

Furthermore, on account of this land of Uḍḍiyāna **[34]** being so very famous, it is shrouded by various fantastic stories. Therefore many people who are ignorant and content with boasts will indeed find it very hard to believe the things I say. In a much earlier period, those who personally journeyed to this region wrote travel accounts. There is no need for me to mention those detailed and accurate travel accounts which exist in other languages, such as that of Sung Yun the T'ang emperor's envoy,[68] and both the Western king Alexander [the Great] (336-306 B.C.E.)

རྒྱའི་བཙུན་པ་ཕ་ཐེན་གཉིས་སོ་ཊ་ཀྱི་ལམ་ཡིག་ཕྲ་ཞིབ་སྐད་རིགས་གཞན་དུ་ཡོད་པ་རྣམས་ནི་སླ་མ་དགོས་ལ། རེ་ཞིག་རང་ཅག་བོད་ཀྱི་ཡུལ་འདི་ནས་ཀྱང་། ད་ལྟའི་མི་ལོ་དགུ་བརྒྱ་ལྷག་གི་སྔོ་རོལ་དུ། རྗེ་ཆོས་ཚང་པའི་བུ་ཆེན་དང་། ཀརྨ་རང་བྱུང་བའི་སློབ་དཔོན་དུ་གྱུར་བ། གྲུབ་ཐོབ་ཨོ་རྒྱན་པ་རིན་ཆེན་དཔལ་དེ། ཟླ་བོ་དཔལ་ཡེ་འབྲིད། དབྱུག་པ་ཕྱུག་ཏུ་ཐོགས། ཞབས་ས་ལ་བཙུགས་ཏེ། འགྲོ་བ་མིའི་ལུགས་སུ་གནས་འདིར་དངོས་སུ་བྱོན་འདུག་པ། དེའི་ལམ་ཡིག་རྒྱས་པ་དང་། དེ་འོག་ལོ་སུམ་བརྒྱའི་རྗེས་སུ་འདིར་བྱོན་པ་སྟག་རས་ངག་དབང་རྒྱ་མཚོ་བ་གཉིས་ཀའི་རྣམ་ཐར་ལ་གཟིགས་དང་། ལམ་བར་གྱི་གྲོང་དང་ཚྭ་ཁ་ལ་སོགས་པ་ཕལ་མོ་ཆེ་ད་དུང་ཡང་ངོས་ཟིན་པ་ཡོད། གཞན་ཡང་གུ་རུ་ལྷོ་ཕྱོགས་པ་སངས་རྒྱས་མགོན་པོ། དར་སེང་པའི་སློབ་མ་རས་པ་རྡོ་རྗེ་དཔལ། རྒྱལ་ཁམས་པ་དཀོན་མཆོག་རྒྱལ་པོ་རྣམས་ཡུལ་འདིར་དངོས་སུ་བྱོན་པ་ཡིན་འདུག་པས། དངོས་སུ་འགྲོ་འདོད་ན་[༡༥] དངོས་སུ་ཕེབས་པ་ཚོའི་གསུང་ལ་མཉན་པར་འཚལ།

མི་འགྲུལ་པའི་ས་རྟགས་གཞན་ནི་ཕར་ཞོག སྔར་གྱི་ལམ་ཡིག་དེ་ཐམས་ཅད་ན་གསུངས་པའི་ཨོ་རྒྱན་གྱི་རི་བོ་ཨི་ལམ་པཐ་ཏ་དེང་སང་ཡང་ཀླ་ཀློ་དང་མུ་སྟེགས་རྣམས་ལོ་ལྟར་འགྲོ་བའི་གནས་ཆེན་ཡིན་པ་འདི་ཀས་ཀྱང་ཆོག གལ་ཏེ་ཁོ་བོས་བདེན་པ་ངོ་སྤྲོད་བྱས་པ་འདི་ལ་ཡིད་མ་ཆེས་ན། ཨོ་རྒྱན་བྱ་བ་དེ་གནས་དང་ས་གར་ཡོད་མི་ཤེས་པ། རི་ཐམས་ཅད་རུས་པ་དང་། ཆུ་ཐམས་ཅད་ཁྲག་ཏུ་འབབ་པ། ཚེ་འདིར་མ་ཟད་ཕྱི་མར་ཡང་མི་སླེབས་པའི་ས་ཞིག་ཏུ་གྱིས་དང་། མི་ཕལ་ཆེར་གྱི་ཁམས་ལ་དེ་འཁྲིད་པར་སྣང་། འོ་ན་གནས་འདིར་མཛལ་ས་ཅི་ཞིག་ཡོད་ཅི་ན། མཐོ་ཡི་རི་བ་དང་ཁྲ་ལམ་མི་བ་ཅི་ཡང་མེད།

མནྟ་ལོར་བྱ་བའི་གྲོང་དེ་ཨོ་རྒྱན་པ་གཉིས་ཀས་གསུངས་པའི་མནྟ་ཕ་རའི་གྲོང་ཡིན།

and the Chinese monk Fa-hsien. From this land of Tibet as well, more than six hundred years before men of the present-day, a few of us, [namely] that great disciple of the master Götsangpa who became the teacher of Karma Rangchungwa (1284-1339),[69] Orgyenpa Rinchenpal, leading his companion Palye[she], carrying stick in hand and with feet planted on the ground, travelled in person to this holy place in the manner of human beings. One who looks into the biography with their extensive travel account, and also into that of Tagre Ngawang Gyatsowa who travelled to this place in their tracks three hundred years later, can recognize again and again, for the most part, such things as the villages along the road and the salt mine. Furthermore, the southern guru Buddhanātha (1514-1610),[70] Repa Dorjepel the student of Darsengpa,[71] and the wanderer Könchog Gyalpo all travelled in person to this land, therefore if you wish to go there in person **[35]** I ask that you attend to what was said by those who actually went there.

As for other unmistakable landmarks, they must be left aside. The [holy] mountain of Uḍḍiyāna, which is mentioned in all those former travel accounts, is Ilamparvata, and it can be permitted also that this very one is the great Tantric site, to which even today barbarians and heretics travel annually [as pilgrims].[72] If you don't believe my introduction of the truth, you will not know where the region of the holy place called Uḍḍiyāna exists. [If one heeds such descriptions of the place as] "All the mountains are of bone and all the rivers flow with blood", it will be turned into a place which is unreachable, not only in this life but in future lives as well, and for most people this is apparently acceptable. But, if one asks whether there are specific sites to visit in this holy place, there is nothing imposing or lucid whatsoever.

That town which is [nowadays] called Manglawar is the village of Mangawar (i.e. Maṅgalapura) which was mentioned by both the Orgyenpas [Rinchenpal and Tagtsang Repa].[73]

རི་ཨི་ཝོའི་སྐད་དུ་ཡོད་པའི་ཕ་བོང་དཀར་པོ་དེ་རྣམས་བྱང་སེམས་ཚོགས་བཅད་ཕྱེད་ཀྱི་ཕྱིར་སྐུ་བཏང་བའི་གནས་དང་། ལུང་སྨད་ཤང་ཀར་རྣར་གྱི་གྲོང་གི་ཉེ་འཁོར་གྱི་མཆོད་རྟེན་ཆེན་པོ་དེ་རྒྱལ་པོ་བྱང་[༣༣]སྤྲོས་བཞེངས་པའི་སྟོན་པའི་རིང་བསྲེལ་གྱི་མཆོད་རྟེན་ཡིན་ཞེས་རྒྱའི་བརྩུན་པའི་ལམ་ཡིག་ཏུ་གསལ། དེ་ལ་སོགས་པའི་མཆོད་རྟེན་རྙིང་པ་ཤིན་ཏུ་མང་ཞིང་། ཡུལ་དེའི་སྐད་དུ་མཆོད་རྟེན་ལ་སྟུམ་པར་འབོད་པས་སྟུམ་པ་རྣམས་ལ་མཇལ་བར་ཞུ། གཞན་ཡང་གྲུབ་ཆེན་པས་ནི་དེ་རྐུ་ཀ་རང་བྱུང་གི་ལྷ་ཁང་དེ་རི་ཞིག་གི་ [༡༦] རྣམ་པར་གཟིང་འདུག་པས། འོ་ན་རི་རྣམས་ལ་ཡང་མཇལ་བར་ཞུ། གནའ་དུས་ཀྱི་མཁའ་འགྲོ་མ་རྣམས་ཀྱི་ཚ་མོ་འཁྲུལ་མེད་ཡིན་ངེས་པའི་དཀར་ལ་དམར་མདངས་ཆགས་པའི་བུ་མོ་མཛེས་མ་ཤིན་ཏུ་མང་པོ་འདུག་པས། དེ་རྣམས་ལ་ཡང་མཇལ་བར་ཞུ། ཨོ་རྒྱན་པས་ཀྱང་དེ་འདྲ་ཞིག་གི་ལག་ནས་ཐུག་པ་ཕོར་གང་བཞེས་ཏེ་རྟོགས་པ་བསྐྱེས་པ་ཡིན། འོན་ཀྱང་བྱ་ཐོང་དགོས་པ་འདི་ཡོད་དེ། དེང་སང་ནི་གནའ་དུས་ཀྱི་མཁའ་འགྲོ་མ་རྡོ་ཚར་འཕེབ་མཁན་རྣམས་ནི་མི་བཞུགས་ཀྱང་། པུཎ་ཛབ་གྱི་ཟླ་སློ་རྣམས་མཚོན་ཆར་ཕབ་སྟེ། ལམ་འགྲུལ་རྣམས་རང་དགར་གསོད་པ་ཡིན་པས། ཅེས་ཀྱང་ཡུལ་འདིར་མ་ཕེབས་པ་འཐད་ཅེས་ལན་བརྒྱར་ཞུས་ལགས། ཡང་ན་ནི་ཡུལ་དེའི་རྒྱལ་པོ་ཧྲ་ཤ་ནས་མགོ་འདྲེན་འཐོབ་པའམ། ཡང་ན་ནི་དཔུང་གྲོང་ཤིན་ཏུ་མང་པོ་སྟེབས་ཏེ་འཐོན་སྲིད་ཙམ་ཡིན་ཡང་ཤིན་ཏུ་ཉེན་ཆེ། དེས་ན་གནས་འདི་ཕྱིན་ཆད་ངོས་ཟིན་པ་དཀའམ་སྙམ་ནས། འདིར་ཙུང་ཟད་ཅིག་བྲིས་པ་ལགས།

མདོར་ན་ཨོ་རྒྱན་ཡུལ་གྱི་ལྗོངས་བཀོད་ཙམ་ཞིག་གཟིགས་པར་འདོད་ན་ནི། མ་ལ་གན་གྱི་བྱང་གི་ལུང་པ་དེའི་ནང་དུ་ཡར་ལ་གཞུང་ཆུ་བརྒྱུད་ནས་ཕེབས་པར་ཞུ།

༣༣) *Orig.* སྤྲོགས།

It is explained in the Chinese monk [Hsüan-tsang's] travel account that "Those white boulders which exist halfway up Mount Ilo (i.e. Ilamparvata) are the holy place where [the Buddha in his former rebirth as a young brahmin] renounced his body for the sake of half a stanza on the aspiration to awakening, and that funerary monument in the environs of the village of Shankardār in the lower valley is the funerary monument with relics of the Teacher which was erected by king Uttarasena."[74] There are a great many ancient funerary monuments such as that, and since they call a reliquary shine a "ghumpa" in the local dialect, one should ask to visit the ghumpas.[75] Furthermore, because a great Tantric adept saw a self-manifested temple of Heruka in the **[36]** form of a mountain there, well, one should also ask to visit the mountains.[76] Because there are a great many pretty girls who appear with fair and glowing complexions, and who obviously are indisputably the granddaughters of the sky-goer goddesses (*ḍākinī*) of former times, one should also ask to visit them.[77] Orgyenpa [Rinchenpal] also received a bowl full of broth from the hands of such a one, and he obtained knowledge.[78] But, for this one needs to give a secret signal. Nowadays, although the sky-goer goddesses of former times, who threw down a rain of stones [on the Tantric adept Lavapa], no longer live there, there are barbarians who are the Pathān who throw down a rain of weapons and kill travellers at their leisure.[79] Therefore, I request you a hundred times please, by all means, do not travel in this area.[80] Either one gets protection from the Bādshāh,[81] the king of the region, or one teams up with a great many companions, and even if it is perhaps possible to proceed the danger is very great.

Because of that, I have written a little here thinking that from now on this holy place might become difficult to identify.

In summary, if you want to see a little of the landscape of the region of Uḍḍiyāna, I suggest you proceed along the central stream of the river up into that valley which is north of Malakand.

གལ་ཏེ་བླ་མ་གོང་མ་རྣམས་ཀྱིས་གང་གཟི་ཊ་པའི་ཡུལ་དེའི་ངོ་མཚར་ཐམས་ཅད་མཐོང་བར་འདོད་ན་ནི། དེར་མ་སོང་བའི་སྔོན་དུ་བྲག་ཕུག་ཞིག་ཏུ་བཞུགས་ལ། སྦྱོར་བ་ཡན་ལག་དྲུག་གི་ཏིང་ངེ་འཛིན་ཡུན་རིང་ [༡༧] དུ་སྒོམ་པར་ཞུ། དེ་འདྲ་གང་ཡང་མ་བྱས་པར། གྲུབ་ཆེན་ལྭ་བ་པས་གང་གཟིགས་པ་རྣམས་རང་གིས་མ་མཐོང་བའི་རྒྱུ་མཚན་གྱིས། གནས་འདི་རྣམས་བརྫུན་མ་ཡིན་ནོ་ཞེས་ཅིས་ཀྱང་མི་གསུང་བར་ཞུ།།

|ཐོག་མ་མེད་ནས་རྟག་ཏུ་འགྲོགས་པ་ཡི།
|མི་འགྱུར་སེམས་ཀྱི་གཤིས་ཀྱང་མི་མཐོང་ན།
|བཙན་ཐབས་སྒོམ་གྱིས་གསར་དུ་བསྐྱེད་པ་ཡི།
|ཡ་མཚན་གྲུབ་པའི་གཟིགས་སྣང་ག་ལ་མཐོང་།

ཞེས་ཀྱང་སྨྲས་སོ།། [༡༨]

[II.II]

||རེལ་ལིའི་གླ་ཆ་དང་གྲུ་ཟན་གྱི་མིང་||

དེ་ཡང་འཆར་ཅན་གྱི་ལམ་བཀའ་བློན་སྤྲུག་དང་། རྡོ་རྗེ་གླིང་ལྷ་བུ་ལ་དང་པོར་སླེབས་པའི་དབང་དུ་བྱས་ན། བཀའ་བློན་སྤྲུག་ནས་ཤི་ལི་གུ་རི་བར་མི་རེ་ལ་མོ་ཊར་གླ་སྒོར་ལྔ་ཅམ་རེ་སྤྲོད། ཤི་ལི་གུ་རི་ནས་ཀ་ལི་ཀ་ཏ་ལ་སྒོར་ ༥ ཨ་ན་ ༡༩ དང་ཀ་ཏ་ནས་གྱ་ཡ་ལ་སྒོར་ ༥ ཡིན། དེ་མིན་ཤི་ལི་གུ་རི་ནས་རྡོ་རྗེ་གདན་ལ་འགྲོ་ན་དང་པོ་ཤི་ལི་གུ་རི་ནས་གྱ་ཡའི་ཊེ་ཀ་ཊ་དགོས་ཤིང་སྒོར་ ༧ སྤྲོད་ཤི་ལི་གུ་རི་ནས་རེལ་ལི་ཞུགས་ཏེ་པར་བ་ཏི་པུར་(PARBATIPUR) དེ་ནས་རེལ་ལི་བརྗེས་ཏེ་ཀ་ཊི་ཧར་(KATIHAR) དེ་ནས་རེལ་ལི་བརྗེས་ཏེ་རེལ་ལི་གཞན་ལ་ཞུ་ཊ་ནས་གཙྪ་བར་དང་དེ་ནས་གཙྪ་འཇའ་ཅོ་ལས་བརྒལ་ཏེ་སླར་ཡང་རེལ་ལི་ལ་ཞུགས་ནས་གྱ་ཡའི་(GAYA) གྲོང་ཁྱེར་བར་དང་།

In case you want to view all the marvels of that region as completely envisioned by the aforementioned lamas, I suggest that before ever going there, you sit in a rock cave and meditate for a long period on **[37]** the [*Kālacakra-tantra* completion stage] concentration of *The Six Branches Combined.* The reason you have not seen the great Tantric adept Lavapa's complete visions of [Uḍḍiyāna] yourself is that you have done nothing at all like that, therefore I ask you absolutely not to state that "These holy places are inauthentic."

It is also said:

> If one has not even perceived the character of immutable mind,
> Which has been ever-present through time without end,
> Where will one perceive the amazingly perfect visions,
> Which are developed anew through rigorous concentration? **[38]**

[ILII.] Rail Fares and Station Names

Furthermore, assuming one arrives initially in somewhere like Kalimpong and Darjeeling on the usual route [taken by Tibetans travelling to India] (see figure 6 & 7): from Kalimpong one pays about 5 *rupees* fare per person for a motorcar as far as Silīguri. From Silīguri to Calcutta [by train] it is 5 *rupees* and 14 *annas*, and from Calcutta on to Gayā it is 5 *rupees*. Otherwise, if one goes to Vajrāsana from Silīguri first one must buy a ticket for Gayā from Silīguri and pay 7 *rupees*. Take the train from Silīguri to Par-ba-ti-pur (PARBATIPUR), then change trains to Ka-ṭi-har (KATIHAR). Then change trains, and having boarded another train as far as the Gangā, and crossing by ship over the Gangā, then take the train once more and go as far as the town of Gā-ya (GAYA).

དེ་ནས་ཤིང་རྟ་ནས་མེ་ལི་ ༥ སོང་ན་རྡོ་རྗེ་གདན་དུ་སླེབས། རྡོ་རྗེ་གདན་གྱི་མིང་ལ་བོ་དྷི་གྷཱ་ཡ་ཞེས་འདྲི་དགོས། ཡང་རྒྱལ་པོའི་ཁབ་ལ་སྐྱོན་དུ་འགྲོ་ན་གནྜ་བཀྲལ་བ་དང་པ་ཏ་ན་ (PATNA) ལ་སླེབས། དེ་ནས་ར་ཛ་གི་རིའི་ཏེ་ཀ་སྐོར་ ༡ ཨ་ན་ ༣ ལམ་ནེ་པ་ཏ་ཆ་ནས་བྷག་ཏྱིཨ་པུར་ (BAKHTIARPUR) དེ་ནས་རེ་ལི་བརྗེ་ནས་གཞན་ལ་ཞུགས་ཏེ་ར་ཛ་གི་རི་ (RAJGIR-KUND) བར་འགྲོ ལམ་ག་ནས་ཨོ་ཏ་ནྟ་པུ་རི་ལ་འགྲོ་ན་བི་ཧར་ཤ་རིབ་ [༣༩] (BIHARSHARIF) བྱ་བའི་གྲུ་ཟན་ནས་བབས། འོན་ཀྱང་མཇལ་རྒྱུ་ནི་ཅང་མེད། ནཱ་ལནྡཱ (NALANDA) ཡང་ལམ་གའི་གྲུ་ཟན་ཡིན། ཡང་རྡོ་རྗེ་གདན་ནས་རྒྱལ་པོའི་ཁབ་ལ་འགྲོ་ན་གྷཱ་ཡ་ནས་མོ་ཏར་ཆེན་པོ་ལ་སྐོར་ ༡ ཨ་ན་ ༨ སྤྲད་ན་བི་ཧར་དང་ནཱ་ལནྡཱ་མཇལ་ཐུབ་ཅིང་། ནཱ་ལནྡཱ་ནས་ཨ་ན་ ༥ སྤྲད་ན་ར་ཛ་གི་རིའམ་རྒྱལ་པོའི་ཁབ་ཏུ་སླེབས།

གྷཱ་ཡ་ནས་བེ་ན་ར་སི་ (BENARES) སྟེ་ཝ་ར་ན་སི་ལ་རེལ་གླ་སྐོར་ ༣ ཨ་ན་ ༤ དེ་ནས་རེ་ལི་བརྗེས་ཏེ་ཨ་ན་གཅིག་གིས་ས་ར་ན་ཐ་ (SARNATH) ལ་སླེབས། དེ་ཆོས་འཁོར་[༣༣]བསྐོར་བའི་གནས་ཡིན།

ས་ར་ན་ཐ་ནས་ཏ་སིལ་དེ་འོ་རིཨ་ (TAHSIL-DEORIA) ལ་ཏེ་ཀ་སྐོར་ ༡ ཨ་ན་ ༤ དེ་ནས་མོ་ཏར་ལ་སྐོར་ ༡ ཨ་ན་ ༨ ཙམ་སྤྲད་ན་མ་ཐ་ཀུ་བར་ (MATHAKUWAR) ལ་སླེབས། དེ་རྩ་མཆོག་གྲོང་ཡིན།

རྩ་མཆོག་གྲོང་ནས་མོ་ཏར་ལ་ཨ་ན་ ༡༣ སྤྲད་ནས་གོ་རག་པུར་ (GORAKHPUR) ལ་འགྲོ དེ་ནས་རེ་ལི་ཞུགས་ཏེ་ནའོ་ཏན་ཝ་ (NAUTANWA) དེ་ནས་རྟ་དང་ཀྲང་ཐང་ཅི་རིགས་ [༤༠] པར་མེ་ལི་བཅུ་གཉིས་སོང་ན། རུ་མིན་དེ་ (RUMINDEI) ལ་སླེབས། དེ་ནི་ལུམྦིའི་ཚལ་ཡིན། ནའོ་ཏན་ཝ་ལ་མ་སླེབས་གོང་ནའོ་གྷར་ (NAUGARH) བྱ་བའི་གྲུ་ཟན་ལ་ཐུག དེ་ནས་བབས་ན་ལུམྦི་ནི་ལ་ཐག་རིང་ཡང་ཤིང་རྟ་དང་མོ་ཏར་ཐོབ།

[༣༣]) *Orig.* བསྐོར།

From there, if one goes 7 miles by horse-drawn cart one arrives at Vajrāsana. One needs to ask for "Bo-dhi-gā-ya" as the name for [the place we Tibetans call] Dorjeden. Further, if one goes first to Rājagṛha, one crosses the Gangā and arrives in Pa-ṭa-na (PATNA). From there buy a ticket to Rājgir for 1 *rupee* and 3 *annas*. As for the route, from Pa-ṭa-na one goes to Bhagtia-pur (BAKHTIARPUR) then, having changed trains and boarded another, go as far as Ra-dzi-gi-ri (RAJGIR-KUND). Along the route, if one goes to Odantapurī one alights at the station which is named **[39]** Bi-har-sha-rib (BIHAR SHARIF), although there is nothing whatsoever [of the ancient monastery] to be seen. For Nālandā (NALANDA) there is also a station on the route. Also when one goes to Rājagṛha from Vajrāsana, if one pays 1 *rupee* and 8 *annas* for the bus from Gayā one is able to visit Bihār and Nālandā, and if you pay 7 *annas* from Nālandā you reach Rājgir or [as we Tibetans call it] Gyalpoé Khab.

From Gayā to Bi-na-ra-si (BENARES), that is, Vārāṇasī, the train fare is 2 *rupees* and 4 *annas*. From there, changing trains one reaches Sa-ra-na-tha (SARNATH) for 1 *anna*. That is the holy place where the wheel of Buddhist doctrine was [first] turned.

From Sārnāth the ticket to Ta-sil-rde'o-ri-a (TAHSIL-DEORIA) is 1 *rupee* and 4 *annas*. If one pays about 1 *rupee* and 8 *annas* for a motorcar from there, one arrives in Ma-tha-ku-bar (MATHAKUWAR). That is Kuśinagarī.

One travels from Kuśinagarī to Go-rag-pur (GORAKHPUR) by paying 12 *annas* for a motorcar. From there one boards a train to Na'o-tan-wa (NAUTANWA). Then if one goes twelve miles, partly by horse and on foot, **[40]** one reaches Ru-min-de (RUMMINDEI). The Grove of Lumbinī (Lumbinīvana) is there. Before arriving in Na'o-tan-wa one reaches a station called Na'o-ghar (NAUGARH), if one alights there, even though Lumbinī is far, one can get a horse-cart and motorcar.

གོ་རག་པུར་ནས་བལ་རམ་པུར་ (BALRAMPUR) ལ་རེལ་ལེའི་ཊི་ཀ་སྐོར་ ༡ ཨ་ན་ ༥ དེ་ནས་མེ་ལི་ལྔ་ལ་ཤིང་རྟ་ནས་སོང་ན་ས་ཧེ་ཊ་མ་ཧེ་ཊ་ལ་སླེབས། དེ་མཉན་ཡོད་ཡིན། སླར་བལ་རམ་པུར་དུ་འོངས་ཏེ། སྐོར་ ༡ ཨ་ན་ ༨ གིས་ཊི་ཀ་ཉོས་ཏེ་ལག་ནཽ་ (LUCKNOW) ལ་འགྲོ

ལག་ནཽ་ནས་སྐོར་ ༣ ཨ་ན་ ༡༠ འི་ཊི་ཀ་བླངས་ཏེ་པ་ཁ་ན་ (PAKHNA) ལ་འགྲོ དེ་ནས་མེ་ལི་འགའ་ཀང་ཐང་ལ་སོང་ན་སངྐིས་ (SANKISA) ལ་སླེབས། དེ་ནི་ལྷ་བབས་ཀྱི་གནས་ཡིན། ཡང་ལག་ནཽ་ནས་སྐོར་ ༥ ལ་མ་ཐུ་ར་ (MUTTRA) བཅོམ་བཀླག་ལ་སླེབས། ལམ་དུ་ཨག་ར་ (AGRA) ཡང་ཡོད།

མ་ཐུ་ར་ནས་སྐོར་ ༡ ཙམ་གྱི་ཌེ་ལི་ (DELHI) ལ་སླེབས། ཌེ་ལི་ནས་སྐོར་ ༩ ཨ་ན་ ༤ ཀྱིས་ཨཾ་འབར་སར་ (AMRITSAR) ལ་སླེབས། ཨམ་འབར་སར་ནས་སྐོར་ ༩ དང་ཨ་ན་ ༣ ལ་འཛོ་གིན་དར་ན་གར་ [༩༡] (JOGINDRA-NAGAR) ལ་སླེབས། དེ་ནས་མོ་ཊར་ནས་སྐོར་གཉིས་ཙམ་ལ་ར་བལ་སར་ (RAWALSAR) མཚོ་པདྨའི་ཐག་ཉེ་ལ་སླེབས།

ཡང་ཨམ་འབར་སར་ནས་ཨ་ན་ ༩ ལ་ལ་ཧོར་དང་དེ་ནས་སྐོར་ ༣ དང་ཨ་ན་ ༣ ལ་ཏག་སི་ལ་ (TAXILA) ལ་སླེབས། དེ་རྡོ་འཇོག་ཡིན། ཏག་སི་ལ་ནས་སྐོར་ ༡ ཨ་ན་ ༧ ལ་པེས་ཤ་ཝར་—(PESHAWAR) ལ་སླེབས། དེ་ཐོགས་མེད་འཁྲུངས་པའི་གནས་ཡིན།

ཡང་པི་ན་ར་སི་ནས་སྐོར་ ༡ ཨ་ན་ ༥ ལ་ཨ་ལ་ཧ་བྷད་—(ALLAHABAD) དང་དེ་ནས་ཨ་ན་དྲུག་གིས་བྷར་ཝ་རི་—(BHARWARI) དང་དེ་ནས་ཨ་ན་ ༡༠ མོ་ཊར་ལས་སོང་ན་ཀཽ་ཤམ་བི་ལ་སླེབས།

པ་ཊ་ན་ནས་སྐོར་ ༡ ཨ་ན་ ༧ ལ་མོ་ཛ་ཕར་པུར་ (MUZAFFARPUR) དང་དེ་ནས་མོ་ཊར་ལས་ཨ་ན་ ༤ ལ་བྷ་ཁ་ར་ (BHAKHRA)དེ་ནས་ཤིང་རྟའམ་ཀང་ཐང་ལ་མེ་ལི་བཞི་སོང་ན་བྷལ་སར་ (BALSAR)ལ་སླེབས། དེར་ཡངས་པ་ཅན་གྱི་ཤུལ་ཙམ་ཡོད། མིང་ལ་སྐར་ཟེར། [༩༣]

From Gorakhpur to Balram-pur (BALRAMPUR) the train ticket is 1 *rupee* and 5 *annas*. If one proceeds with a horse-cart for five miles from there, one arrives at Sa-he-ṭa-ma-he-ṭa (i.e. Saheṭh-Maheṭh). That is Śrāvastī. One returns to Balrāmpur again, and buying two tickets for 1 *rupee* and 6 *annas* one travels to Lag-nau (LUCKNOW).

From Lucknow take a 2 *rupee* and 10 *anna* ticket and go to Pa-kha-na (PAKNHA). Then, if one proceeds on foot for a few miles one arrives at Sangkisa (SANKISA). That is the holy place of [Buddha's] descent from the [realm of the] gods. Also from Lucknow one reaches Ma-thu-ra (MUTTRA) (i.e. Mathurā), Chomlag [in Tibetan], for 5 *rupees*. Āgra (AGRA) is along the route as well.

From Mathurā one reaches Deh-li (DELHI) for about 1 *rupee*. From Delhi one reaches Am-'bar-sar (AMRITSAR) for 4 *rupees* and 8 *annas*. From Amritsar ones reaches 'Jo-gen-dar-na-gar (JOGINDRA-NAGAR) **[41]** for 4 *rupees* and 3 *annas*. From there by motorcar one gets close to Ra-bal-sar (RAWALSAR), Tsho Pema [in Tibetan], for about 2 *rupees*.

In addition, from Amritsar it is 4 *annas* to La-hor (i.e. Lahore), from where one reaches Tag-si-la (TAXILA) for 3 *rupees* and 2 *annas*. That is Dönjog [in Tibetan]. From Taxila one reaches Pis-sha-war (PESHAWAR) for 1 *rupee* and 7 *annas*. That is the place where Asaṅga was born.

In addition, from Benares it is 1 *rupee* and 5 *annas* to A-la-ha-bā-da (ALLAHABAD) and from there 6 *annas* to Bhar-wa-ri (BHARWARI). Then if one goes by motorcar one reaches Kauśāmbī for 10 *annas*.

From Patna it is 1 *rupee* and 7 *annas* to Mo-ja-phar-pur (MUZAFFARPUR), and then by motorcar on to Bha-kha-ra (BHAKHRA) it is 8 *annas*. If one proceeds about 4 miles by horse-cart or on foot from there one arrives at Bhal-sar (BALSAR). In that place there exist some remains of Vaiśālī, named Ghara. **[42]**

མོ་ཛ་ཕར་པུར་ནས་སི་གོ་ལི་ (SAGAULI) བར་སྐོར་ ༡ ཙམ་དང་དེ་ནས་ཨ་ན་ ༨ ལ་བེ་ཏྟི་ཧ་ (BETTIAH) ལ་སླེབས། དེར་དྲི་མེད་ཀུན་ལྡན་གྱི་ཕོ་བྲང་ཡོད་ཟེར། མོ་ཛ་ཕར་པུར་ནས་རག་སོལ་ (RAXAUL) བར་སྐོར་ ༡ ཨ་ན་ ༡༣ དེ་ནས་བལ་ཡུལ་གྱི་ས་མཚམས་ཡིན།

ཡང་ཤི་ལི་གུ་རི་ནས་རག་སོལ་ལ་ཤར་གྱིས་སོང་ན་སྐོར་ ༤ ཨ་ན་ ༡ ཡིན། ཡང་ཤི་ལི་གུ་རི་ནས་པར་བ་ཏི་པུར་དང་དེ་ནས་སྐོར་ ༩ ཨ་ན་ ༤ སྤྲད་ན་ གོ་ཏ་ཏི་ (GAUHATI) ལ་སླེབས། དེ་ནས་མེ་ལི་བཅུ་བདུན་སོང་ན་ (མཀྣུ་ཞེ) ཤར་ རྩ་མཆོག་གྲོང་ཡོད།

ཡང་པ་ཏ་ན་ནས་སྐོར་ ༣ ལ་སུལ་ཏན་གན་ཛི་ (SULTANGUNJ) ལ་ སླེབས། དེར་བིཀྲམ་ལ་ཤི་ལའི་ཤུལ་ཙམ་ཡོད། དེ་ནས་ཨ་ན་ ༩ ལ་བྷ་གལ་ པུར་ (BHAGALPUR) དུ་སླེབས། དེ་ཉི་ཟ་ཧོར་གྱི་རྒྱལ་ཁམས་ཛོ་བོ་འཁྲུངས་ པའི་གནས་ཡིན། གནས་འདི་གཉིས་ཀ་ལི་ཀ་ཏར་འགྲོ་བའི་ལམ་ཡིན།

ཀ་ལི་ཀ་ཏ་ནས་སྐོར་ ༨ ཨ་ན་ ༡༣ ལ་ཙི་ཏ་གོང་ (CHITTAGONG) ལ་ སླེབས། ཀ་ལི་ཀ་ཏ་ནས་འཛའ་ཙི་ལམ་སྐོར་ ༡༥ ལ་འབར་མའི་མཆོད་རྟེན་ལ་ སླེབས། [༩༣]

ཀ་ལི་ཀ་ཏ་ནས་ཁ་རག་པུར་ (KHARAGPUR) དེ་ནས་བེ་ཟ་ཝ་ད་ (BEZWADA) དེ་ནས་གུན་ཏུར་ (GUNTUR) དེ་ནས་མོ་ཏར་ལ་སྐོར་གཅིག་གིས་ ཧྣ་ན་ཀོ་ཏ་ (འབྲས་སྤུངས་) ལ་སླེབས། འོན་ཀྱང་ཆེ་ཡོར་རེ་བ་ཙི་ཡང་མཐོང་ རྒྱུ་མེད། དེ་ནས་ཤིང་རྟ་ལ་སྐོར་གཉིས་སྤྲད་ན་ནགར་ཛི་ན་ཀོ་ཏ་ལ་སླེབས། དེ་ ལྷོ་ཕྱོགས་དཔལ་གྱི་རི་སྐྱེ་མཛལ་རྒྱུ་ཡང་མང་།

ཀ་ལི་ཀ་ཏ་ནས་གུན་ཏུར་བར་སྐོར་ ༡༨ ཨ་ན་ ༡༠ སླར་གུན་ཏུར་ནས་སྐོར་ ༡༠ ཨ་ན་ ༡༣ ལ་ཏེ་ཀ་སླངས་པས་མེ་ཏེ་ར་སིའི་གྲོང་ཁྱེར་བརྒྱུད་ནས་ར་མེ་ཤྭར་ (RAMESWAR) ལ་སླེབས། དེ་ནས་འཛའ་ཙི་ལ་སྐོར་ ༥ ཙམ་སྤྲད་ན་སིངྒ་ལ་རུ་ སླེབས། དེར་སྐོར་ཉི་ཤུ་ཙམ་ལ་ཀན་ཌི་དང་ཨནུ་ར་རྡ་པུ་ར་གཉིས་སོགས་བསྐོར་ཐུབ།

From Muzaffarpur it is about 1 *rupee* as far as Si-rgo-li (SAGAULI), and from there one reaches Bi-te-ha (BETTIAH) for 6 *annas*. It is said the palace of Drimé Kunden exists there. From Muzaffarpur on to Rag-sol (RAXAUL) it is 1 *rupee* and 12 *annas*, and after that is the Nepalese frontier.

In addition, from Silīguri if one goes directly to Raxaul it is 7 *rupees* and 1 *anna*. Also if one goes from Silīguri to Parbatipur, and pays 4 *rupees* and 7 *annas* from there, one reaches Gho-ha-ṭi (GAUHATI). From there, if one proceeds 17 miles, there is Mahāmuni, the eastern Kuśinagarī.

In addition from Patna one reaches Sul-tan-gan-ji (SULTANGANJ) for 2 *rupees*. In that place are some remains of Vikramaśilā. From there for 4 *annas* ones gets to Bha-gal-pur (BHAGALPUR). That is the region of Zahor, the place where Atiśa was born. Both these holy places are on the road which goes to Calcutta.

From Calcutta one reaches Ci-ṭa-gong (CHITTAGONG) for 7 *rupees* and 12 *annas*. From Calcutta one gets to the funerary monuments of Burma by ship for 15 *rupees*. **[43]**

From Calcutta to Kha-rag-pur (KHARAGPUR), Be-za-wa-da (BEZWADA) and then Gun-tur (GUNTUR) [by rail], and then for 1 *rupee* by motorcar from there, one arrives at Dhanakoṭa, Drepung [in Tibetan]. However, those hoping for great things will not see anything here. If one pays 2 *rupees* for a horse-cart from there one gets to Na-gar-ji-na-ko-ṭa (i.e. Nāgārjunikoṇḍa). South of there is Śrīparvata, and [in that place there is] still much that could be visited.

From Calcutta to Guntur it is 16 *rupees* and 10 *annas*, and by taking a 10 *rupee* and 12 *anna* ticket once again from Guntur, one arrives in Ra-me-shwa-ra (RAMESWAR) after passing through the city of Madras. If one pays about 4 *rupees* for the ship from there, one gets to Ceylon. There one is able to make a tour which includes both Kandy and Anurādhapura for about 20 *rupees*.

ཡང་ཨ་ལ་ཧ་བ་ད་ནས་ཨ་ན་ ༡༢ ལ་ཨ་ཛོ་དྷྱ་ (AJUDHYA) ལ་སླེབས། དེ་ནི་དགའ་བྱེད་རཱ་མ་འཁྲུངས་པའི་གནས་ཡིན།

ཡང་ལག་ནཽ་ནས་འཇན་སི་ (JHANSI) དེ་ནས་བྷེ་ལ་ས་ (BHILSA) དེ་ནས་སན་ཅི་(SANCHI) ལ་སླེབས། དེར་སྒྱུ་ངན་མེད་ཀྱི་མཆོད་རྟེན་ངོ་མཚར་ཅན་ཡོད། སན་ཅི་ནས་བྷོ་པལ་ (BHOPAL) དེ་ནས་འཇལ་སྒོན་ (JALGAON) ལ་སླེབས། [༩༤] ལག་ནཽ་ནས་འཇལ་སྒོན་བར་བསྡོམ་སྐོར་ ༡༠ ཨ་ན་ ༦ ཡིན། འཇལ་སྒོན་ནས་མོ་ཊར་ལ་སྐོར་ ༣ ལ་ཨ་ཛན་ཏ་ལ་སླེབས། དེ་ནས་ཨཽ་རང་ག་བད་ (AURANGABAD)བར་མོ་ཊར་ལ་སྐོར་ ༢ དེ་ནས་མོ་ཊར་ལ་ཨ་ན་ ༡༢ སྤྲད་ན་ཨེ་ལོ་རའི་ཕུག་བར་སླེབས། སླར་ཨཽ་རང་ག་བད་ནས་རེ་ལི་ཞུགས་ཏེ་མན་མད་ (MANMAD) དེ་ནས་ཀལྱན་ (KALYAN)སླེབས། དེ་ནས་ལུ་ན་བ་ལ་ (LONAVALA) དང་དེ་ནས་མེ་ལི་གསུམ་སོང་ན་ཀར་ལི་ཕུག་བར་སླེབས། སླར་ཀལྱན་ནས་ནཱ་སིཀ་ལ་སླེབས། ཨཽ་རང་ག་བད་ནས་ནཱ་སིཀ་བར་སྐོར་ལྔ་ཙམ་འགྲོ ཀལྱན་ནས་ལུ་ན་བ་ད་བར་ཨ་ན་ ༨ ཡིན།

ཡང་སྔར་ལམ་གྱི་བྷོ་པལ་ (BHOPAL) ནས་ཨུ་ཛེན་ (UJJAIN) ལ་སྐོར་ ༢ ཨ་ན་ ༡ ལ་སླེབས། དེ་ནི་འཕགས་རྒྱལ་ཡིན། དེ་ནས་འཇལ་སྒོན་བར་སྐོར་ ༣ ཨ་ན་ ༡༥ དང་དེ་ནས་སྔར་ལྟར་ཨ་ཛན་ཏ་སོགས་འགྲོ་ཐུབ།

ཡང་གོང་དུ་བཤད་པའི་ཀ་ལི་ཀ་ཏ་ནས་འབྲས་སྤུངས་ལ་འགྲོ་བའི་ལམ་དུ་ཁུར་ད་ (KHURDA) ཟེར་བའི་གྲུ་ཟན་ནས་རེ་ལི་བརྗེས་ན་པུ་རི་ (PURI) ལ་སླེབས། དེ་ནི་ཨོ་ཊི་བི་ཤ་སྐེ་དེར་ [༩༥] གྲོང་ཁྱེར་དང་ཛ་གད་ན་ཐ་བྱ་བའི་ཁྱབ་འཇུག་གི་ལྷ་ཁང་ངོ་མཚར་ཅན་དེ་ཡོད། ཀ་ལི་ཀ་ཏ་ནས་པུ་རི་བར་སྐོར་ ༦ ཙམ་མོ།

འདིར་གླ་ཆ་ཁྲིམས་པ་དག་ནི་དུས་ཐོག་གཅིག་གི་ཐོབ་ཐང་ལ་ཆ་བཞག་པས་མཐའ་གཅིག་ཏུ་ངེས་པ་མེད། དེ་ཡང་སྔོད་ས་དམའ་ཤོས་ཁོ་ནའི་གླ་ཆ་ཡིན། སྔོད་ས་ཨང་གཉིས་པ་སོགས་ལ་སུམ་འགྱུར་བཞི་འགྱུར་གྱིས་གླ་ཆེ་བ་ཡོད། ཐག་རིང་གི་ཏེ་ཀ་ཏོ་ཐུབ་ན་ཆུང་ཁེ་པོ་ཡིན།

Also from Allahābād one reaches A-dzo-dhya (AJUDHYA) (i.e. Ayodhya) for 12 *annas*. That is the place where joyous Rāma was born.

Also from Lag-nau (i.e. Lucknow) via 'Jan-si (JHANSI) and then Bhil-sa (BHILSA) (i.e. Vidiśā), one reaches San-ci (SANCHI). In that place there is a marvelous funerarymonument of Aśoka. From Sāñcī via Bho-pal (BHOPAL) one reaches 'Jal-ghon (JALGAON). **[44]** From Lucknow as far as 'Jal-ghon it is a total of 10 *rupees* and 6 *annas*. From Jālgaon one gets to A-jan-ta (i.e. Ajaṇṭā) by motorcar for 2 *rupees*. From there it is 2 *rupees* as far as Au-rang-ga-bad (AURANGABAD) by motorcar, and then if one pays 12 *annas* for a motorcar one arrives at the caves of Ellorā. Once again, from Aurangabad one boards the train for Man-mad (MANMAD) and then arrives in Kalyan (KALYAN). From there one goes to Lu-na-ba-la (LONAVALE) and then if one proceeds for 3 miles one reaches the Kar-le (i.e. Kārli) caves. Once again, from Kalyan one gets to Bhom-bhe (i.e. Bombay). One goes from Au-rang-ga-bad as far as Bombay for about 5 *rupees*. From Kalyan as far as Lonavale it is 9 *annas*.

In addition, from Bho-pal (BHOPAL) on the previous route one gets to U-jen (UJJAIN) for 2 *rupees* and 1 *anna*. That was [the historical city of] Ujjayinī. From there is it 3 *rupees* and 15 *annas* as far as Jālgaon and, as before, from there one is able to go to such places as A-jan-ta.

In addition, from the railway station which is called Khur-da (KHURDA) on the route which goes from Calcutta to Dhanakoṭa as explained above, if one changes trains there one arrives in Pu-ri (PURI). That place is Oḍiviśa, **[45]** and there is a city there and a wonderful temple of Viṣṇu which is known as Dza-gad-na-tha (i.e. Jagannātha). From Calcutta as far as Pu-ri it is about 6 *rupees*.

Because the fares which are recorded here are based on what was current at only one time, they will continue to change. Furthermore, the fares are only for the lowest class of seat. In the second class seats, and so on, the fares are three and four times higher. If one is able to purchase a long-distance ticket it is slightly cheaper.

[II.III]

དེ་ལྟར་རྒྱ་གར་གྱི་གནས་ཆེན་འདི་དག་ངོས་ཟིན་པ་དཀའ་བ་མ་གཏོགས། འགྲོ་ཐབས་རང་ཉིད་དེང་སང་གི་ལུགས་ལམ་དང་མོ་ཊར་སོགས་ལ་བརྟེན་པས་དེ་ཙམ་དུ་དཀའ་བ་མ་ཡིན། རྒྱ་གར་གྱི་ལོ་རྒྱུས་ཧར་ཆེ་བ་འབའ་ཞིག་རྣ་བར་འཇགས་པ་རྣམས་ཀྱིས་ཉེ། རྣ་བས་ཐོས་པའི་ལྡིར་སྒྲ་དང་། མིག་གིས་མཐོང་བའི་ཛ་ཆུང་གཉིས་ཆ་མ་མཚུངས་པའི་དབང་གིས། ཐམས་ཅད་ལ་ཐེ་ཚོམ་སྐྱེས་ཏེ། རྡོ་རྗེ་གདན་དངོས་བཏགས་གཉིས། ཕྱ་ར་ཊཱ་སི་ཆེ་ཆུང་གཉིས་སོགས་རྒྱུན་མའི་གཡོ་གཏམ་དེ་ཀ་སྒྲ་བའི་མགོ་རྩུགས་མོད། ད་ལྟའི་རྒྱ་གར་འདི་རྒྱ་གར་ངོ་མ་དེ་ཡིན་ཕྱིན། གནས་ཆེན་འདི་དག་ཀྱང་དེ་དང་དེ་ངོ་མ་ཡིན་པ་ལ་ཐེ་ཚོམ་མི་དགོས། ལར་བདག་རང་ཡང་ཐོས་ཚད་ལ་ཡིད་ཆེས་པའི་བླུན་པོ་ཅིལ་ཆུང་ཞིག་མ་ཡིན་གྱི། རང་བཞིན་ [༩༧] གྱིས་དབང་པོ་རྣོ་ཞིང་། མི་ཚེ་ཐོས་པ་ལ་བསྐྱལ་བའི་སྤྲང་པོ་དཀྱིད་ལྡན་ཞིག་ལགས་པས། གང་སྣྲས་འདི་ཀུན་ལ། ནོར་བ་དང་ཁྲུངས་མེད་པ་དང་མགོ་བསྐོར་བའི་དོགས་པ་སུམ་ཆར་ཡང་མ་དགོས་པ་ལགས་མོད། མིའི་རིགས་ཕལ་མོ་ཆེ་ཞིག་ལ་ནི་དཀའ་བ་ཞིག་སླ་རུ་བཏང་སྟེ་བཤད་ན་ཡིད་མི་ཆེས་ཤིང་བརྣས་ཚོས་བྱེད། དེ་ལས་སླ་མོ་ཞིག་དཀའ་རུ་བཏང་སྟེ་བཤད་ན་མཁས་པར་བརྩི་[༣༤] ཞིང་ཡིད་ཆེས་བྱེད་པར་འདུག་པས་བྱ་ཐབས་ཟད།

[II.IV]

ལམ་ཡིག་འདི་བདག་རང་རྒྱ་གར་དུ་འཁོད་དེ་ལོ་བཅུ་གཉིས་ལྷག་སོང་སྐབས་སྟར་གྱི་བྲིས་པ་དེ་ལ་བསྟོན་མ་ཕུང་ཟད་བཏབ་སྟེ་རྒྱས་སུ་བཏང་བ་ཙམ་ལགས་སོ།

།སྙིང་རྒྱས་རི་བོའི་ནགས་སུ་བཙོམ་ལྡན་འདས།
།མཉམ་བཞག་གཡོ་མེད་སྐྱིལ་[༣༥] མོ་ཀྲུང་མཛད་དེ།

---

༣༤) *Orig.* བརྩེ།
༣༥) *Orig.* དཀྱིལ།

[ILIII. Conclusion]

So, except for the difficulty of identifying these great holy places of India, since one can rely upon such things as present-day railroad and motorcars the mode of travel [to them] is itself not difficult at all. Those who allow only very boastful histories of India into their ears have doubts about everything due to the disparity between the roar of thunder heard by the ears and the tiny drum seen by the eyes, and this is indeed the starting point for the uttering of nothing other than continuous deceptive rumours, such as [those about] both the real and the false Vajrāsana, or both the large and the small Vārāṇasī! Since this India of the present-day is the real India, there is no need to doubt that these great holy places are certainly the real ones. Moreover, I myself am not just a silly fool who believes everything he hears. **[46]** My senses are naturally keen, and I am an astute beggar who spent his life listening, therefore even the three doubts about things being mistaken, baseless and contrived in all I have related are certainly unnecessary. When something difficult is made simple and then explained, the majority of people are skeptical and dismissive. On the other hand, when something simple is made difficult and then explained one is considered a scholar and given credence, so there is nothing to be done!

[ILIV. Colophon and Concluding Verse]

I myself wrote this guide-book in India over twelve years ago. Small additions have been made to what I wrote on that former occasion, and it has been expanded.

> Lord [Buddha] sat cross-legged in unwavering
> concentration,
> In the forest of the broad-topped hill.

།གང་ཞིག་གཟིགས་པའི་ཟབ་མོའི་བདེན་པ་དེ།
།མ་ལུས་འགྲོ་ལ་མངོན་དུ་འགྱུར་བར་ཤོག།

།གོ་འཕང་གང་ཞིག་ཁམས་གསུམ་སྐྱེ་རྒུ་འདིའི།
།ཚིག་དང་བློ་དང་དཔྱོད་པའི་ཡུལ་མིན་པ།
།གང་དུ་བདེ་བར་གཤེགས་པ་གཤེགས་གྱུར་པའི།
།ཞི་བའི་ས་དེ་མྱུར་དུ་བརྙེད་པར་ཤོག ། [༩༧]

སྟོན་པ་སྨྲ་ངན་ལས་འདས་ནས་ཉིས་སྟོང་བཞི་བརྒྱ་གྱ་དགུ་པ་ལ། རྒྱལ་ཁམས་བསྐོར་བའི་ཨ་མདོ་དགེ་འདུན་ཆོས་འཕེལ་གྱིས་བྲིས་པའོ།། །།

[ILV]

།།མ་ཧཱ་བོ་དྷི་སོ་སཡི་ཊེ་སངས་རྒྱས་པའི་འདུས་པ་ཆེན་པོ།།

འདི་ཉིད་ཐོག་མར་དཔལ་དྷརྨ་པཱ་ལས་བཙུགས་ཤིང་། ཙ་བའི་གནས་གཞི་ཀ་ལི་ཀ་ཏ་དྷརྨ་ར་ཛི་ཀའི་གཙུག་ལག་ཁང་དང་། གྲོས་པའི་ཡན་ལག་ནི་རྡོ་རྗེ་གདན། ཕར་ཀཱི།
ཌྷེ་ལི། མཏྲས། ཨཛྨེར་སོགས་རྒྱ་གར་གྱི་ཡུལ་གྲུ་དུ་མ་དང་།
དབྱིན་ཡུལ་ལོན་ཌོན། འཛར་མན་ཕྲར་ལིན། ཨ་མི་རི་ཀ ཉེའུ་ཡོར་ཀ གཞན་ཡང་ཧོལ་ལན་སོགས་ཕྱིའི་རྒྱལ་ཁབ་དུ་མར་ཡང་གཙུག་ལག་ཁང་སོགས་མཆིས་སོ།

ཅེས་ཀྱང་ནང་པ་སངས་རྒྱས་པ་རྣམས་ཀྱིས་རང་བསྟན་མི་ཉམས་གོང་འཕེལ་གྱི་ཆེད་དུ་ལུས་སྲོག་ལོངས་སྤྱོད་ལ་མ་ལྟོས་པའི་འབད་པ་རྩལ་འདོན་དགོས་པ་འདི་ཡིན་ལ། རེ་ཞིག་འདི་ཀའི་མ་ཧཱ་བོ་དྷི་ནས་གང་གྲུབ་པ།

དགེ་སློང་མཁས་པ་རྣམས་ཕྱིའི་རྒྱལ་ཁབ་སོ་སོར་བཏང་སྟེ་འཆད་རྩོད་རྩོམ་པའི་ཆོས་ཀྱི་ཕོ་ཉ་རྒྱུན་མ་ཆད་པ། [༩༨]

May any profound truth which he perceived,
Become a reality for all beings!

Any state of enlightenment has no object which can
be analyzed
With the words and thoughts of sentient beings from
the three realms.
May that place of tranquility where the Sugata has
gone
Be rapidly obtained! **[47]**

Written by Amdo Gendun Chöphel, who wandered around the countries, two thousand four hundred and eighty nine [years] after the Teacher passed beyond suffering.

[ILV. Appendix:] The Maha Bodhi Society, A Great Union of Buddhists

This [Society] itself was initially founded by Śri Dharmapāla. The Calcutta headquarters is the monastic centre of Dharmarājikā, and as for the separate branches, they include monastic centres in many regions of India, such as Vajrāsana, Vārāṇasī, Delhi, Madras and Ajmer, and in many foreign countries as well, such as those at London in England, Berlin in Germany, New York in America, and also in Holland.

Buddhists should certainly firmly strive, without regard for life and property, in order to advance, unimpaired, their own teachings, and this is what has been accomplished by the Mahābodhi [Society] in a short time:

Learned, fully-ordained monks have been sent out individually to foreign countries, and they are emissaries who teach, debate and write the Buddhist doctrine continually. **[48]**

ཡོ་རོ་ཞི་དྲུག་གི་རིང་ཟླ་རེ་བཞིན་དབྱིན་སྐད་དུ་བསྒྱུར་བའི་ཆོས་ཀྱི་སྤྲིང་ཡིག་པར་འདེབས་ཀྱིས་བཀྲམ་བཞིན་པ།

ཕར་ཀློསིར་སྒོར་ཉིས་འབུམ་ལྷག་གིས་རིང་བསྲེལ་སྙིང་པོར་བཅས་པའི་གཙུག་ལག་ཁང་བཞེངས་པ།

སྒོར་ ༡༠༠༠༠༠ འགྲོ་སོང་གིས་སྡེ་སྣོད་གསུམ་རྒྱ་གར་འཕྲུལ་སྐད་དུ་བསྒྱུར་ཞིང་པར་བཏབ་པ། དབྱིན་ཡུལ་དུ་གཙུག་ལག་ཁང་དང་དགེ་འདུན་གྱི་སྡེ་བཙུགས་པ་འདི་དག་རགས་རིམ་ཙམ་དང་། གཞན་ཡང་དོ་རྗེ་གདན་བྲམ་ཟེའི་དབང་ལས་བླངས་ཏེ་སངས་རྒྱས་པས་བདག་གིར་བྱེད་པའི་སྤྱད་ཁྲིམས་གཏུགས་བྱེད་མུས་དང་།

ལྷ་བབས་ཀྱི་གནས་སུ་མགྲོན་ཁང་བརྩིགས་པ། ལྟུགས་པར་ལས་ཁྲུངས་འཛུགས་པ། སྨན་ཁང་དང་སྨན་སྦྱིན་གྱི་སྲོལ་རྒྱས་སུ་གཏོང་པ། ཀ་ཏའི་གཙུག་ལག་ཁང་ལ་སྟོན་པའི་རྣམ་ཐར་གྱི་ལྡེབ་བྲིས་བྲི་བ་སོགས་བྱ་དགོས་ཀྱང་ཤིན་ཏུ་མང་བས། བསྟན་པ་དང་སྟོན་པ་གཅིག་པའི་ཆོས་ཀྱི་གྲོགས་རྣམས་ནས་འདི་ཀའི་ཚོགས་འདུའི་མཆན་བཞེས་པ་སོགས་རོགས་རམ་གང་དྲག་གནང་རྒྱུའི་བཀའ་དྲིན་མི་ཆུང་བ་མཁྱེན་ཞུ།

ཚའི་ཚོ་ར་འདུའི་མཆན་བཞེས་པར་ཞལ་འདེབས་སྒོར་ ༣༥༠ དཀྱུས་[36] མའི་ཞལ་འདེབས་ལོ་ལྟར་སྒོར་ ༡༡།།

[36]) *Orig.* བཀྱུས།

Each month for forty-six years they have spread [the teachings] by founding a newsletter about Buddhist doctrine which is translated into English.

With more than 200,000 *rupees* they erected a monastic centre at Vārāṇasī which contains essential relics [of the Buddha].

By spending 200,000 *rupees* they have sown the seeds for a translation of the *Tripiṭaka* into Hindi. They established a monastic centre and a community of monks in England. Generally these [things have been done], and furthermore they have taken Vajrāsana from the control of the brahmins, and are engaged in legal action for the purpose of giving [lawful] possession of it to Buddhists.

And, they constructed a guest-house at the holy place of [Buddha's] descent from the gods [i.e. Sāṃkāśya]. They established a printing office. They have expanded the practice of providing free clinics and medicines. Because there is a great deal which still needs doing, such as painting the murals of the Teacher's biography in the monastic centre at Calcutta, I request from all friends of the Dharma with the same doctrines and Teacher, no small kindness in giving any possible help, including taking up membership of this society.

There is a 250 *rupee* donation for taking up life membership of the society; 11 *rupees* is the ordinary annual donation.

Notes to the Translation

1. Our author is paraphrasing here from the *Mahāparinirvāṇa-sūtra* in the Tibetan *Vinaya* (cf. the edition by Waldschmidt 1951:389-391, 41.5-7, 41.9).
2. That is, Bhāvaviveka's *Madhyamaka-hṛdaya-vṛtti-tarkajvālā* (Peking 5256). It is to be noted that a version of the Sanskrit *kārikā*-s of the *Tarkajvālā* were among the finds of the 1936 Sankrityayan manuscript collecting expedition in Tibet. Gendun Chöphel does not indicate which *Tarkajvālā* text he is referring to here, but see Kawasaki (1992) on variations between the Sanskrit and Tibetan materials. Gendun Chöphel also cites the *Tarkajvālā* in his other works, e.g. see *gTam-rgyud* 1:181.
3. This is a departure from both the literary and popularly accepted scheme of the eight important sites of the Buddha's life. Here the author replaces the name of Vaiśālī with that of Nālandā. The enumeration in the Tibetan version of the *Aṣṭamahāsthānacaityastotra* (*gNas chen po brgyad kyi mchod rten la bstod pa*, Peking 2024) has Vaiśālī (Yang-pa-can) at this point, with the gloss: *sku tshe 'du byed btang ba las // slar yang sku tshe byin brlabs pa*, the last part of which is similar to Gendun Chöphel's *sku tshe byin gyis rlabs pa* here. A different canonical version with the same title (Peking 2025) also mentions events at Vaiśālī at this point. The Chinese *Pa-ta-ling-t'a-ming-hao-ching* also gives Vaiśālī at this point (Nakamura 1980:261; cf. also Huntington & Huntington 1990:531-533), and a review of fourteen (mainly Tibetan) sources on the different schemes of eight great *stūpa* shows Nālandā is omitted in all cases (Pema Dorjee 1996:11-16). Gendun Chöphel perhaps made the change influenced by the Pāli tradition of the names of the six great cities, which replaces Vaiśālī with Kosambī, or did so due to the greater importance of Nālandā for the Tibetan tradition and is simply in error. As Templeman (1999:188) notes, Nālandā was "an almost obligatory reference in the biographies of [earlier] Tibetans visiting India."

Compare the section on Vaiśālī below (pp.24-5), which does not even mention it as a frequent resort of the Buddha.

4. On the replica Mahābodhi temples in Burma, Thailand and Nepal see Snellgrove (1978:417-422; pls. 337-340) and Leoshko (1988:102-132). The replica Mahābodhi temple (*rdo-rje-gdan-gyi zhing-gi bkod*) at Patan was reported in an early 19th century Tibetan guide to Nepal (Wylie 1970:2, 18, n.29). On Tibetan substitutes for the major sites of the Buddha's life in eastern India, see Huber (forthcoming). On the Tibetan identifications of Kuśinagarī and other major Buddhist sites in Assam see note 40 of the Translator's Introduction herein.
5. On Chag Lotsawa's account see Roerich (1959) and Champa Thupten Zongtse (1981). The "extensive account of Vajrāsana" by Chomden Rigpé Reldri is so far unknown, although Jackson (1989:223-224) has catalogued a text in the Bihar Research Society collection at Patna (and therefore known to Gendun Chöphel) entitled *Register and Guide for Vajrāsana* (*rDo rje gdan gyi dkar chag dang lam yig*) and of unknown authorship (Jackson no.1510, BRS bundle no.590). It is possible that Gendun Chöphel took this to be Chomden Rigpé Reldri's account.
6. Gendun Chöphel describes both these models, one of black stone and one of wood, in more detail in his account of his visit to Narthang monastery (*gTam-rgyud* 1:34). Sankrityayan also illustrated and described them after his third expedition to Tibet (1937:17-18, plates between p.16-17), cf. Oldham (1937); and see also Rowland (1938), Guy (1991) and Leidy & Thurman (1997:54, plate), and Weldon & Singer (1999:46-47) on the existence of other such models.
7. Although normally Tibetan *gan-dho-la* is the same as *dri-gtsang-khang* (*gandhakuṭa*; also *gandhālaya*), "perfumed chamber" or "place of perfumes", it seems best here to translate *gan-dho-la* with "*caitya*-temple" as it is used both as a term and a proper name by Tibetans to refer specifically to the Bodh Gayā Mahābodhi temple and other buildings whose architecture closely resembles it. See, for instance, Waddell (1905:229-230) on the Gyantse Kumbum; and cf. Ricca & Lo Bue (1993:302). Our author's use of the term *gan-dho-la/li* here and elsewhere appears to be derived from Chag Lotsawa, as does *dbu-rtse* (Roerich 1959:13, 14).
8. Concerning the origins of the Mahābodhi temple, the author was clearly familiar with both the Tibetan tradition as given in Chag Lotsawa (Roerich 1959:65-70) and many later histories (Sørensen 1994:497-499) and that of Hsüan-tsang and the colonial archaeologists who attributed the earliest temple-building to Aśoka (Cunningham 1892:4).

9. The author's time-frame here refers to the apocryphal inscription of Amaradeva dated 948, which was first used as historical evidence by Cunningham (1871b:6-7) but then rejected in his final report of 1892. To arrive at his date for the Burmese restorations Gendun Chöphel could have followed Cunningham's 1871 report (but not the 1892 report where he opts for the 11th century, pp.27-29, 75-77) or the later revision of Cunningham by Barua (1931-1934, vol.1:208-210).
10. This reconstruction (as opposed to renovation), funded by the Government of Bengal, was carried out between 1880 and 1884, and therefore at least 50 years before Gendun Chöphel could have first visited the site.
11. This attribution is not attested in the non-Tibetan sources, and while Tibetan authors such as Chag Lotsawa (Roerich 1959:65), Butön (Obermiller 1932:125) and Tāranātha (Lama Chimpa & Chattopadhyaya 1970:107-108) mention various works of Nāgārjuna at the site, this is not among them.
12. This is slightly ambiguous since *bre* is also the Tibetan colloquial term referring to the square *harmikā* of the reliquary shrine housing the relics; as a dry measure 1 *bre* = approximately 1.5kg.
13. This is mentioned twice by Chag Lotsawa (Roerich 1959:65, 71). Accounts of the transfer of the famous "twelve-year old" Jowo Śākya image to Lhasa are well-known in later Tibetan histories; Sørensen 1994:66-72).
14. This Tibetan attribution first occurs in Chag Lotsawa (Roerich 1959:65). In contrast, Hsüan-tsang and the colonial archaeologists attributed some of the railings to Aśoka (Cunningham 1892:11-16). It is to be noted that none of the surviving pillar and railing inscriptions from the site attribute them to Nāgārjuna, but to a variety of other, particularly female, Śuṅga dynasty donors dating back to the 2nd century B.C.E. (Barua 1931-1934, vol.2:65-76). Our author's use of the term *rdo'i dra-mig* for the railings here and elsewhere appears to be derived from Chag Lotsawa (Roerich 1959:14).
15. The author here refers to the many bas-reliefs on the stone railings and pillars enclosing the circumambulation path. These include faces in the centre of lotus medallions which Cunningham (1892:14) identified as king's heads and "grotesque faces" (cf. 1892:plate IX; 1871b:plate XI). Barua (1931-1934, vol.2:90-91) later identified others of these as signs of the solar zodiac, in particular the female bust of Kanyā (plate 43). Chag Lotsawa associated Tārā with the site of Vajrāsana (Roerich 1959:65, 70, 74-76) and Cunningham

(1871b:11) noted a ruined temple called "Tara Devi" on his 1861 visit.

16. Chag Lotsawa (Roerich 1959:71-72) only noted a much-worshipped pair of Buddha foot-prints on a stone block, which seems to be the same as the "Buddha-pad" later described by Cunningham (1871b:9-10, plate VII).

17. This is in error. Since Hsüan-tsang's time there have been eighteen carved lotus 'footprints' along the Buddha's promenade or *caṅkrama* (Beal 1884, II:122; Cunningham 1892:8-10; Barua 1931-1934, vol.2:25-27).

18. During her pilgrimage to Bodh Gayā in late 1930-31, Rinchen Drolma Taring "[P]ointed to the antique stones, which she said were the remnant of a burning ghat where Tibetan visitors, on completing their pilgrimage, were wont to sacrifice a part of their hair." (Byron 1933:323).

19. This clearly refers here to the well-known *stūpa* of Animiṣa (or Animiṣalocana) where the Buddha is said to have "gazed unblinkingly" on the Bodhimaṇḍa in the second week after his awakening. To date I have been unable to trace this rather environmentally destructive narrative in the classical Buddhist sources. However, a text passage on aspects of the Buddhist Tantric geography of India by Jamyang Kyentse Wangpo (1820-1892) has an almost identical narrative element in its section on Bodh Gayā, in the context of a discussion of various *stūpa* at the site: "In that [place], when our Teacher attained buddhahood, the other trees which were not Bodhi Trees were incinerated by rays of light. And still today, if one proceeds east a little from the Bodhi Tree there exists a life-size image of the Buddha and above it the so-called Light Emanation Caitya-temple" ('Jam-dbyangs mKhyen-brtse'i dBang-po 1977:69b, l.2-3). I am grateful to Dan Martin for this reference.

20. *A-kar* > *a-ga-ru*, the *agaru* tree, *Amyris Agallocha* or *aguru* the fragrant Aloe tree (*Aquilaria Agallocha*), Monier-Williams, *Sanskrit-English Dictionary*, 4-5; *Bod-rgya*, v.3:3115 under *a-ga-ru* has "a fragrant tree." (*dri-zhim ljon-pa*)

21. The account of Bodh Gayā by Jamyang Kyentse Wangpo also briefly mentions this otherwise unidentified tree: "At the south-western boundary of Vajrāsana is a handsome tree which grew as an offshoot [lit. "branch"] of the Bodhi Tree, called the A-gar Bodhi" ('Jam-dbyangs mKhyen-brtse'i dBang-po 1977:70b, l.4-5). In relation to what Gendun Chöphel has written here, a story about the Bodhi Tree in Hsüan-tsang, whose account he resorts to frequently, is of interest:

Prior to his conversion, Aśoka orders that the Bodhi Tree be burnt, only to find a new tree miraculously sprouting up from the site of the fire, and which is called the "ashes Bodhi Tree" (Beal 1884:II, 117).

22. See Roerich (1959:73).

23. This contradicts the location given by Chag Lotsawa (Roerich 1959:85), who visited it to the northwest of Nālandā in the 13th century. Furthermore, below (p.12) Gendun Chöphel also locates another site with the same name, although not a charnel ground, near Rājagṛha. Gendun Chöphel and George Roerich's translation of the *Blue Annals* has the Buddha going to "Maghada to the Śītavana grove" to meet and teach king Bimbisāra shortly after his enlightenment, at a location between Bodh Gayā and Rājagṛha (Roerich 1976:20). However, in the early sources this meeting takes place at the Supratiṣṭhacaitya near the Nairañ-janā River (Lamotte 1988:17). Gendun Chöphel and Roerich have used "Śītavana grove" to render the original Tibetan *btang brang gi tshal* ('Gos Lo-tsā-ba 1984, I:41).

24. Here the author is following the story related in Chag Lotsawa (Roerich 1959:78-80). The traditional number in the Buddhist literature is eighty-four thousand *stūpa*.

25. The word *gru-zan* used throughout for "station" is the author's phonetic equivalent for the English loan word "station" in India, which is often pronounced "istashin" in Urdu or Hindi.

26. Its destruction by the Turks was discussed in *gTam-rgyud* 1:388-389.

27. See Roerich (1959:85).

28. Tsang Nyön Heruka's biographies of both Milarepa and Marpa Lotsawa relate the story of how Nāropa bowed three times towards Tibet, and the hills of Pulahari likewise inclined towards Tibet and remained that way (Lhalungpa 1977:82; Nālandā Translation Committee 1982:90).

29. Cf. Beal (1884, II:170) "...priests, to the number of several thousand..."

30. The author's "New Rājagṛha" here is apparently derived from the Chinese pilgrims' accounts or more likely from archaeologists of Indian Buddhism who, beginning with Cunningham (e.g. 1871b), also followed the Chinese usage. Fa-hsien mentions the "New Rājagṛiha,—the new city which was built by king Ajātaśatru" (Legge 1886:81; cf. Beal 1884:lviii) to distinguish it from Bimbisāra's "old" city (Legge 1886:82), which Hsüan-tsang later identified as Kuśagarapura (Beal 1884, II:149). However, the old Indian name

for Rājagṛha as the "mountain-fenced" capital of Magadha, and which is found in the Sanskrit epics, is Girivrāja.

31. An account of how Bābā Jagat Singh, the Dewān of the Rāja of Vārāṇasī Chait Singh, partially demolished the *stūpa* in 1793-94 to obtain building materials for Jagatganj was related by Cunningham (1871b:113-118). These facts where then widely reported in early 20th century Maha Bodhi Society publications.
32. The Pañcavargika, being Ājñāta Kauṇḍinya, Aśvajit, Vāṣpa, Mahānāman and Bhadrika, the Buddha's first five disciples and former mendicant companions at Uruvilvā.
33. Following Cunningham (1871b:117) and Narain (1937:11), this refers to the upper octagonal tower built by Akbar in 1588 to commemorate his father Humāyūn's visit to the site.
34. Our author neglects to mention that there were actually three sets of Buddha relics housed in the Mūlagandhakuṭī Vihāra. In addition to those he mentions from Taxila and Nāgārjunikoṇḍa (see notes 35, 36, and 38 below), a third set extracted from a *stūpa* at Mirpur Khas by H. Cousens iṇ 1910 was presented by the Government of India to the Maha Bodhi Society on November 10th, 1935, and enshrined on the 4th anniversary of the opening of the Vihāra (Blakiston 1935:563-566).
35. Relics from Taxila were presented by the Government of India to the Maha Bodhi Society on November 11th 1931, at which time they were deposited in the base of the Buddha's statue in the Society's new Mūlagandhakuṭī Vihāra during its inauguration. The relics were one of Sir John Marshall's finds from the Chir Tope of the Dharmarājikā grouping, complete with stone outer casket, silver inner casket, and gold relic box plus a silver scroll with Kharoṣṭhī inscription dated to the 1st century A.D. which states they are relics of the Buddha (Anon 1931:521).
36. Relics from Nāgārjunikoṇḍa were presented to the Maha Bodhi Society by the Government of India on December 27th, 1932, on the first anniversary of the opening of the Mūlagandhakuṭī Vihāra (Anon 1933).
37. The Tibetan *rin po che'i ga bu* (>*ga-bur or -pur*?) here is unclear. It could refer to some type of crystalline gemstone, cf. Das, *Tibetan-English Dictionary*, p.204, *ga-bur, sting-zil-ga-bur* is a kind of stone like *pho-cong-sting-zil*; *Bod-rgya*, v.3:2859, *shel-ga-bur*, a type of white camphor resembling pieces of blue ice. Or, *ga-bu* here refers to the inner phials or miniature caskets, made of crystal or beryl,

which actually held the bone relics of the Bhaṭṭiprolu *stūpa* (see note 38 below), and thus our text intends "a gemstone relic phial".

38. The author's account is confused here. He has confounded data on two separate relic finds, both of which were eventually given to the Maha Bodhi Society. The Nāgārjunikoṇḍa relics mentioned here were discovered by A.H. Longhurst at the site of the great *stūpa* in 1927. The relics were originally deposited in a tiny, round gold container placed in turn within a miniature, silver *stūpa*-like casket which was inside a larger, broken earthen pot (Anon 1930:126-128; Daya Ram Sahni 1933:1-4). On the basis of nearby inscriptions the find was dated to about the third century C.E. (Longhurst 1931, 1933, 1935). There was no explicit epigraphic evidence to identify the relics as being those of the Buddha. Gendun Chöphel's description here can only refer to the relics and inscribed stone casket discovered in 1891 at the great *stūpa* of Bhaṭṭiprolu, some 80km to the east of Nāgārjunikoṇḍa. The stone casket inscriptions, dated by Bühler to about 200 B.C.E. (Rea 1894:iv), state explicitly that the relics are of the Buddha. A distinct characteristic of the Bhaṭṭiprolu find is the use of an outer, inscribed stone receptacle, and two inner ones being of crystal and beryl (Rea 1894:9-14, plates I-IV). These same relics were presented to the Maha Bodhi Society by the Government of India and duly enshrined in the new Dharmarājikā Vihāra at the Calcutta headquarters on November 26th 1920 (Anon 1920:257-259). This appears to be what the author is describing here.

39. This refers to the regular anniversary celebrations of the building and consecration of the Mūlagandhakuṭī Vihāra, at which time the Maha Bodhi Society publicly exhibited the collection of Buddha relics enshrined there for worship. Although our author has the correct month for the anniversary celebration (the Vihāra was opened on November 11th 1931), the festival was in fact irregular. For example, the first anniversary was staged from 27th-29th December 1932 in order to accommodate Buddhist pilgrims from outside India who wished to attend (Anon 1932:1).

40. This refers to Raja Baldeodas Birla and Seth Jugal Kishore Birla, the Indian donors of the Maha Bodhi Society's Sārnāth *dharmaśālā* (Anon 1937:80-83).

41. Cf. the original inscription in Hultzsch (1969:164-165).

42. The now century-old debate over Piprāhwā and Tilaurakot as candidates for the site of ancient Kapilavastu remains unsettled, see Chakrabarti (1988:109-112) and Härtel (1991:70-80).

43. Our author's identification of both the Buddha and the "well" (*khron-pa*) are in error here. A pillar fragment with the Kanakamuni inscription is associated with the site of Nigliva, although this is problematic as it has been known since its discovery not to lie *in situ* (Härtel 1991:73-74). The Buddha name confusion probably relates to the fact that Kanakamuni (Tibetan: gSer-thub) is often found in name lists together with Krakucchanda in the texts.
44. Śāriputra and Maudgalyāyana, the Buddha's "model" disciples.
45. In fact Hsüan-tsang (and Fa-hsien) did not mention an elephant capital for this pillar, but a lion, cf. Beal (1884, I:203) "..a stone column about 70 feet high which was erected by Aśôka-râja...Above it is a lion sitting on his haunches." A full discussion of how the Chinese pilgrims misidentified the actual elephant capital for a lion was given by Cunningham (1871b:277-278) and perhaps Gendun Chöphel made his statement here on the basis of this.
46. The site is discussed in detail in the *gTam-rgyud* 1:109-112.
47. He does, however, discuss it in the *gTam-rgyud* 1:411.
48. The author's calculation in clearly in error: In 1937 it had been four hundred and sixty-eight years since Guru Nānak's birth (1469) and three hundred and ninety-eight years since his death (1539). The error was first criticized by Geshe Sherab Gyatso (Shes-rab rGya-mtsho 1984:30).
49. Rangrig Repa (17th-18th cent.), a yogin of the Drukpa Kagyü school, was a native of Spiti whose travels in northwest India included Jālandhara (Ehrhard 1991:13).
50. The identification of Tsho Pema by pilgrims as Padmasambhava's miraculous lake mentioned in the later Nyingmapa hagiographical literature appears to be quite late, perhaps dated to the late 18th- or early 19th century only. It is first mentioned as a place of Tibetan pilgrimage in the 1850s and 1860s (see Havnevik 1999: 141-145, 153, 185). Other sites in the region were also given the same identification, including the Golden Temple in Amritsar and also Lahore (see Tucci 1940:14; Bharati 1978:82; Combe 1926:173). Although nowadays claimed as an important site revived by Tibetan exiles from the 1950s on, in Gendun Chöphel's own day Tsho Pema was, according to the eye-witness accounts of Buddhist pilgrims, totally neglected (e.g. Siriwardhana 1933:511). This is no doubt why he only mentions it in passing here, and one further reason why the long passage on Tsho Pema in the heavily edited 1968 Dalhousie edition of the *Guide to India* must be dismissed as an interpolation.
51. See Bu-ston (1966:57, 5).

52. Bu-ston (1966:57, l.5) states: "In a long recess down in the meditation cave, there is a stone *liṅga*, a symbol which resembles the knee [of the hypostatic *vajrakāya*]."

53. The travel account of Tagtsang Repa Ngawang Gyatso used by Gendun Chöphel mentions the site of Maru one day travel further down the Chenab Valley from Triloknāth (i.e. in Tibetan: Re-'phags, or Ras-'phags, on which see Schubert 1935a), and that in the scheme of twenty-four Tantric sites it corresponds to the toes of the hypostatic *vajrakāya* (Tucci 1940:72). Our author is clearly referring here to the site of Markuladevī at Udaipur.

54. For most Tibetans the Drimé Kunden (Dri-med Kun-ldan) referred to here is a prince character in a popular Tibetan opera (A-ce lHamo) narrative of the same name which is closely based upon the Buddhist story of prince Sudhana's sacrifice in the *Viśvantara Jātaka* (see Bacot 1914).

55. Our author uncritically accepts the old confusion of identity that the Land of Li (Li-yul) was Nepal (Bal-yul, i.e. Kathmandu Valley for Tibetans) rather than Khotan. Interestingly, in his later historical work the *White Annals* he devoted a half page to refuting just such an identification as being false (dGe-'dun Chos-'phel 1990a:224; cf. *gTam-rgyud* 1:39), presumably after picking up Western scholarly refutations of this identification (cf. Thomas 1935:3-38; Brough 1948) from his orientalist contacts in India, studying Dunhuang documents, or by accepting the more critical assessments of other earlier Tibetan authors, such as the Fourth Khamtrül Tenzin Chökyi Nyima (1730-1779) (Macdonald & Dvags-po Rin-po-che 1981:103) or the Tsenpo Nomonhan (1789-1838) (Wylie 1970:19-20).

56. In the *Blue Annals* (*Deb ther sngon po*) this difference of orthography based upon Tibetan and Indian pronunciations is given several times ('Gos Lo-tsā-ba 1984, I:65, 297). The east Indian (Bengal) location of Zahor, followed here by our author, is described in both Sarmapa and Nyingmapa histories of the Tantras. In the 14th century hagiographies of Padmasambhava, Zahor became identified in the northwest of India, in order to equate it closely with Uḍḍiyāna. Later Tibetans popularly identify Zahor as the town and region of Mandi in Himachal Pradesh.

57. The word *'ja'-tsi* used throughout for "ship" is the author's phonetic equivalent for the Urdu *jhāj* or *jahāz*, derived from the Arabic *jahāzī*.

58. Our author published a separate essay on the life and travels of Varnaratna in *The Maha Bodhi* (see Lama Geshe Chömphel 1941).

59. Some Tibetan traditions hold this to be the site where the *Kālacakra-tantra* was first preached, and elsewhere (*gTam-rgyud* 1:117-122) Gendun Chöphel discusses it at length. Other Tibetan sources locate Dhānyakaṭaka in eastern India, and this question has been extensively discussed by Macdonald (1970), who used this and other passages in the *Guide to India* in her review.
60. This refers to the Esala Perahera festival staged annually in Kandy to celebrate, amongst other things, the Buddha's tooth relic kept in the city.
61. This passage, with one word altered and in verse format—a layout I have opted for here—was also used by the author at the conclusion of his translation of the *Dhammapada* from Pāli into Tibetan (completed in Kulu, 1944) (dGe-'dun Chos-'phel (1990b:270); it was, however, edited out of the recent Tibetan edition and English translation (dGe-'dun Chos-'phel 1985:206-207).
62. According to Buddhaghosa's *Manorathapūraṇī*, they came from the city of Asitañjana (Strong 1995:46-7) while Lamotte (1988:66), citing a Chinese source, states that they were from Bactria and returned to build the first *stūpa* there; cf. von Hinüber (1989:114) on the name Bhallika in relation to the city Bahlika (Balkh).
63. Śāntigupta was a teacher of Buddhaguptanātha (1514-1610). Buddhism seems to have disappeared from Java around 1500, although Buddhaguptanātha claims to have met śrāvakas of the "Sendhapa order of monks" and Tantric teachers there in what must have been the mid- to late 16th century (Templeman forthcoming: 551, 1.2-3).
64. Tibetan *drug* "six" here is clearly in error for *gsum* "three" as the actual monument has only three distinctive circular upper terraces. This is clear evidence that the author, as most of his biographers suspect, did not himself visit the site.
65. This description, with virtually identical wording, occurs in *gTam-rgyud* 1:121.
66. The author's equation of this name with the modern region of Cambodia is problematic with this spelling. The Sanskrit name for the 9th-13th century Khmer state was Kambuja-deśa. The Kamboja commonly listed in the Buddhist Sanskrit texts was one of the sixteen "Great Countries" (*mahājanapada*) under Āryan influence in about the 5th-6th cent. B.C.E., referring to both a country and people located in South-western Kashmir and Kāfiristān. In later Thai texts the name Kamboja was used to designate the 11th century Lavo kingdom which was a dependency of Angkor. It was also used as the

name for one of the Shan states in northern Burma (Rispaud 1966:220-222, map).

67. In the section on Atiśa in the *Blue Annals* (*Deb ther sngon po*) the name Gyanag Tongkun Gyelpo is found ('Gos Lo-tsā-ba 1984, I:297), which Roerich and Gendun Chöphel rendered as "the king sToṅ-khuṅ (Tongking, Indo-China) of China" (Roerich 1976:241). Cf. *Bod-rgya* II:1107: "The king of eastern China is called *tūng kus* in Chinese."

68. The author is mistaken with regard to both period and person here. Sung Yun was dispatched to collect Buddhist literature in India by the Wei Empress a full century before the beginning of the T'ang dynasty in 618.

69. That is, the Third Karmapa Rangchung Dorje.

70. Cf. the account by Tucci (1931).

71. This likely refers to the Drukpa Önpo Darma Senge (1177/8-1237) and Repa Dorje, on whom see rTa-tshag Tshe-dbang-rgyal (1994:663-664).

72. Cf. Stein's account (1929:168-171) of a visit to the summit of the mountain which also mentions both Muslim and Hindu (i.e. "barbarians and heretics") pilgrimage to the site.

73. Cf. the same identification of the two in Stein (1929:76).

74. Cf. the passages from Hsüan-tsang in Beal (1884:123-4, 126), but also those in Stein's account (1929:49-50, 169) of Swāt from which the author appears to have derived his wording here. Photographs of both the Uttarasena *stūpa* at Shankardār and the flat, white rocks on the summit of Mount Ilam are also found in Stein (1929:plates 21 & 97).

75. Stein (1929:26) made the same point when discussing the 'Gumbats' or 'domes' of old *stūpa* sites in his account of Swāt.

76. This is also related in the narrative of Tagtsang Repa Ngawang Gyatso's visit to Swāt (Tucci 1940:81).

77. Both the accounts of Swāt by Orgyenpa Rinchenpal and Tagtsang Repa Ngawang Gyatso continually refer to local women as being *ḍākinī* (Tucci 1940). Gendun Chöphel took up the issue of Swāt women as *ḍākinī* again in the *gTam-rgyud* 1:138-139. In his manual of erotic love, the *'Dod pa'i bstan bcos,* Gendun Chöphel surveys the sexual expression of women throughout India, including specific comments about those from Uḍḍiyāna; see Hopkins & Yuthok (1992:206-207).

78. Here the author refers to the incident in Orgyenpa Rinchenpal's account of a visit to Swāt (Tucci 1940:55; cf. Roerich 1976:701).

79. Here the author refers to a story about the stoning of the Tantric siddha Lavapa related in Orgyenpa Rinchenpal's account of a visit to Swāt (Tucci 1940:52).
80. This is also related in the narrative of Tagtsang Repa Ngawang Gyatso's visit to Swāt, when a teacher named Buddhanātha urges the Tibetan pilgrim not to visit the area as he would be killed by the Pathān there (Tucci 1940:78).
81. Once again, the author repeats the same points made in Stein's (1929) report on Swāt. Stein himself managed his successful 1926 tour of the area only because of his political connections with the powerful ruler of Swāt, the Bādshāh Miāngul Gul-shāhzāda, and travelled everywhere under the protection of the Bādshāh's 'men-at-arms'. It is highly unlikely that Gendun Chöphel enjoyed any such privilege.

Appendix A

Tibetan Versions of the *Guide to India*

This appendix contains a descriptive listing, ordered by publication date, of all the main versions of the Tibetan text available. I felt it worthwhile to provide this because there has been some confusion in the secondary sources about the status of the original text and its various later editions:

—1939. *rGya gar gyi gnas chen khag la 'grod pa'i lam yig. Guide to Buddhist Sacred Places in India.* Calcutta, Maha Bodhi Society. Note: This version was announced as *A Guide to Buddhist Sacred Places in India* ("in Tibetan with several maps"), by the Maha Bodhi Book Agency in issues of *The Maha-Bodhi* for 1940 (48:1-48:8, January-August). The cover of this version, dated 1939, was reused for the 1945 expanded version of the text printed in Gangtok in 1950. Despite an extensive search of libraries and archives, this edition has not been seen by me nor any of my informants to date.

—Tibetan xylographic version? Stoddard (1985a:330) states: "....Tethong avait commandé la gravure des blocs du *Lamyig* avec ceux du *Dhammapada* á Nyemo (Tsang), mais Gedun Ch'omp'el fut arrêté et les blocs furent laissés sur place. Il n'est pas certain que les blocs xylographiques aint été imprimés."

—1950. *rGya gar gyi gnas chen khag la 'grod pa'i lam yig. Guide to Buddhist Sacred Places in India.* Gangtok, Sikkim

Government Press, pp.48 printed, 3 original maps, frontispiece photo of a monk praying at the entrance to the Mahābodhi temple. On the inside back cover is a statement by a Maha Bodhi Society editor printed in Tibetan: *Ma hā bo dhi so sayi ṭe las kyi gtso bo rgya gar du bstan pa slar 'dzugs pa dang gnas chen rnams nyams gso byed pa 'di yin cing / slar nas 'dri rtog gang bzhed rigs 'di ka'i spyi khyab las 'dzin de pa pi ya—ba la sing ha la phyag bris gnang bar zhu //.* Note: This is the expanded version on which all later editions and reprints are based.

—1968. *rGya gar gyi gnas chen khag la bgrod pa'i lam yig. Guide to Buddhist Sacred Places in India*. Dalhousie, edited and printed by Ḍa-hor Blo[-bzang] Rab[-rgyas], pp.61 handwritten. Reprinted 1968 in Dharamsala. Note: It is this version that Stoddard (1985a:330) has chosen to list in her L'oeuvre publiée section of Gendun Chöphel's works, however this is misleading. Even a cursory comparison of it with the 1950 Gangtok printing shows that they are radically different. Apart from a dozen or so selected lines of text, the first seven and a half original pages have been omitted from the beginning of this version. Some of this original text is then later inserted between pages 25-30. A large part of the original text is then reproduced, albeit with errors added, but the original section on Nepal and most of the section on Ceylon are then omitted. The entire section on the twenty-four Tantric sites and Swāt Valley is also omitted. The original railway prices and station names section is retained, although inserted before it is a long passage from a version of the *Ma ṇi bka' 'bum*. The text concludes with two long extracts (pages 49-61) concerning the sites of Maratika in Nepal and mTsho Padma in Himachal Pradesh, the latter quoted mainly from the *Padma bka' thang*. These are clearly not the work of Gendun Chöphel, as already considered by A.W. Macdonald

(1985:11). The original maps have all been poorly redrafted and modified by some unknown artist or scribe.

—1976. *rGya gar gyi gnas chen khag la bgrod pa'i lam yig / dge 'dun chos 'phel gyis mdzad pa'o // Guide to Buddhist Sacred Places in India by dGe 'dun chos 'phel*. New Delhi, Tre-hor gDong-thog bsTan-pa'i rGyal-mtshan, pp.48 printed, 3 original maps, frontispiece photo of general view of Mahābodhi temple. Reprinted 1984 in Delhi. Note: Although Stoddard (1985a:330) states that this edition was "révisée par T.C. Dhongthog", it was not and is in fact an exact photo-offset reproduction of the 1950 Gangtok printing, only minus the original title page, the frontispiece and the rear inside cover statement. A short publisher's preface in cursive Tibetan preceeds the text.

—1984. *rGya gar gnas chen khag la bgrod pa'i lam yig mdo smad pa dge 'dun chos 'phel nas brtsams pa bzhugs so //. A Guide Book to the Holy Places of India by Amdowa Gendun Chhephel*. Sarnath, Sushil Printing Press, pp.63 printed. Note: The original Indian railway prices and station names section is deleted and replaced by a simple table of kilometer distances between certain main stations. Seven lines of prose text and two lines of verse are also omitted, as are the original maps. Minor spelling changes or misprints have been introduced throughout the text. All of the original apparatus of English and Indian scripts, underlining, and so forth, has been removed. The original second paragraph on page 45 of the 1950 Gangtok printing has been exchanged for one written by a later editor. A short editorial statement in Tibetan preceeds the main text, explaining that the book was reprinted due to the demand created by a great increase in the numbers of Tibetan pilgrims visiting Indian Buddhist sites.

—1989. *rGya gar gyi gnas chen khag la bgrod pa'i lam yig bzhugs so*. In: *mKhas dbang dge 'dun chos 'phel gyi gsung rtsom phyogs sgrig*. Chengdu, Si-khron Mi-rigs dPe-skrun-khang, 1989, pp.351-395. Note: This edition reads very close to the 1950 Gangtok version, yet it contains many misspellings of place names in foreign languages, and introduces minor variations of Tibetan wording and spelling. The last two lines found in the 1950 Gangtok printing are omitted in this one. All words in Devanāgarī script have been deleted, as have the original maps, front cover, frontispiece and rear cover statement.

—1990. *rGya gar gyi gnas chen khag la bgrod pa'i lam yig bzhugs so*. In: *dGe 'dun chos 'phel gyi gsung rtsom*, vol. 3. (Comp. & Ed.) Hor-khang bSod-nams dPal-'bar, Lhasa, Bod-ljongs Bod-yig dPe-rnying dPe-skrun-khang (Gangs-can Rig-mdzod, 12), pp.311-351, and reprinted 1994 in Lhasa. Note: Another version like the 1989 Chengdu edition, with minor editorial changes and a slightly different layout.

—1998. *rGya gar gnas yig bdus pa*. In: *gNas yig phyogs bsgrigs*. (Eds.) dGe-'dun Chos-'phel, *et. al.* Chengdu, Si-khron Mi-rigs dPe-skrun-khang, 1998, pp.340-382. Note: Another edited version like the 1989 Chengdu and 1990 Lhasa editions, this one missing the entire last section with the Maha Bodhi Society appeal.

—Works based on the *Guide to India*: See gZhis-rtse Ri-kha (1985), whose text is based mainly upon quotes from or paraphrases of the *Guide to India*. Another work of unknown authorship possibly closely based upon the *Guide to India* is entitled: *rGya gar 'phags pa'i yul du nang ba'i mchod rten dang gnas mchog byin can rnams kyi bshad pa mthong thos kun grol*, published in Kalimpong by G. Tharchin, 1956, 124pp. booklet in printed Tibetan. This work is listed in the Library of Tibetan Works and Archives holdings (*dKar-chag*:229, LTWA no. Ka-13728), but upon enquiry with the LTWA it was described as "missing".

Appendix B

Index of Inscriptions on Gendun Chöphel's Maps in the *Guide to India*

The following index lists all inscriptions on Gendun Chöphel's three original maps published in the *Guide to India* (see figures 3, 4, and 6). I have included them for completeness since they contain many place names not mentioned in the text of the *Guide to India* itself, and also because the original maps are difficult to read and do not reproduce well. The indexes follow Tibetan alphabetical order. Gendun Chöphel's original spellings, in italics, are listed first in the form represented on the maps, the use of brackets and upper case English lettering being preserved as per the author's usage on the maps. Following these, where appropriate, translations and/or identifications are given within brackets in plain script.

Inscriptions on Map 1 (figure 4)

Title: *rGya gar nye yul dang bcas pa'i rnam pa lam tsam bsdus te bkod pa'i sa khra* [Map which Sets Out a Rough Outline Form of India Together with Neighbouring Countries].

Kamarupa [Kāmarūpa]
Ka-li-ka-ta [Calcutta]
Kalingga [Kaliṅga]

sKya-nar-bu [Pāṭaliputra]
Kha-che [Kashmir]
Ganggā [River Gangā]
Gamdha-ra [Gandhāra]
rGya-nag [China]
sGra-ngan [=sGra-mi sNyan-pa, i.e. Kuru]
lNga-len [Pañcāla]
rDo-rje-gdan [Vajrāsana]
Nas-gling [Dhānyadvīpa, i.e. Java]
Bal-yul [Nepal]
Bod-gangs-can [Tibet]
Byang-lam [Uttarāpatha, Northern Region]
Bhanggal [Bengal]
Bhar-ma [Burma]
Bhombhe [Bombay]
'Bigs-byed [Vindhya]
Malaya [Malaya]
Yangs-pa-can [Vaiśālī]
Yamuna [Yamuna River]
Yun-nan [Yunnan]
Ran-gun [Rangoon]
Li-yul [Khotan]
Shyam (Siyam) [Siam]
Sindhu'i yul [Land of Sindhu]
Singgala [Ceylon]
gSer-gling [Suvarṇadvīpa, i.e. Sumatra]
lHo-dpal-gyi ri [Southern Śrīparvata]
lHo-phyogs rgya-mtsho [Southern Ocean, i.e. Bay of Bengal]
lHo-phyogs Ma-la-ya'i ri [Southern Hill of Malaya, i.e. Malayagiri]
lHo-lam [Dakṣiṇāpatha, Southern Region]
Aphakanistan [Afghanistan]
O-rgyan [Swāt Valley]

Inscriptions on Map 2 (figure 3)

Title: *rGyal po'i khab kyi ljongs bkod nges 'dzin tsam* [Landscape of Rājagṛha From Memory]

Grong-skyer-gyi rgyal-sgo'i shul [Traces of the Royal Gates to the City, i.e. the Hastināpura Gate]
Bya-rgod phung-po'i ri-bo [Gṛdhrakūṭaparvata, i.e. Vulture's Peak]
rGyal-po'i khab-kyi grong-skyer chags-pa'i shul [Traces of the City Foundations of Rājagṛha]
Chu-bo dByangs-can-ma [Sarasvatī River]
Nag-po rtsegs-pa'i ri [Hill of Kālaśilā]
Bhar-ma'i mgron-khang [Burmese Guesthouse]
Ma-skyes-dgra'i pho-brang-gi shul [Traces of Ajātaśatru's Palace]
Tshu[>*Chu*]*-tshan* [Hot Spring]
Ri-bo sKya-bsang[*s*] [Pāṇḍugiri]
Sumagadhi'i rdzing-bu [Sumāgadhā's Pool]
bSil-ba'i-tshal [Sītavana]
'Od-ma'i-tshal [Veṇuvana]
'Od-srung-phug [Kāśyapa's Cave]

Inscriptions on Map 3 (figure 6)

Crest Caption: *Rgya gar 'phags pa'i yul / mchod rten ring bsrel kyi snying po can bzhugs pa'i zhing* [The Holy Land of India. The field where there exist the reliquary shrines possessing a core of (the Buddha's) relics]

Lower Caption: *Yul gyi dbus gtso bor gyur ba'i rgya gar gnas chen khag la bgrod pa'i rel lam sa khra 'di chos 'phel gyis bris* [This map of rail routes for travelling to Indian holy places which have become the most important in Madhyadeśa was drawn by (dGe-'dun) Chos-'phel]

Kalikata
Kalyan
Kar-le
Katihar
Ki'ul, KIUL
Koshambi (Ko-sam)
bKa'-blon-sbugs
sKya-nar-bu (Paṭṇa)
Kha-che (Ka-shi-mir)
Khagaria, KHAGRIR
Khan-do-ba, KHANDWA
Khur-da, KHURDA
Ga'onpur, GAWNPUR
Gaya
Guntur
Gon-da, GONDA
Ghohati
Gho-rag-pur
rGyal-po'i-khab
Ci-ta-gong
bCom-brlag (Ma-thu-ra)
Cha-pu-ra, CHUPRA
'Jal-ghon
'Jo-gin-darna-gar
mNyan-yod (Saheṭ-mahet)
Tasil-de'o-riya
Dhe-li
rDo-'jog (Tag-si-la)
rDo-rje-gling
rDo-rje-gdan (Bo-dhi-ga-ya)
gNas-bcas (Ayodhaya)
Nalandā
Na'o-rgar
Na'o-tan-wa

Pakh-na
Par-ba-ti-pur
Pa-thankoṭ, PATNAKOT
Pisha-war, Thogs-med 'Khrungs-sa
Pha-rukhabad, FARUKHABAD
Phe-ran-dha
'Phags-rgyal (U-jen)
Balaram-pur
Betia, Lus-'phags (Dri-med Kun-ldan-gyi pho-brang)
Be-za-bha-da
Bikramashila
Bhagalpur, Jo-bo 'Khrungs-sa
Bhagnepur
Bhag-tia-pur
Bhaṭni
Bhi-na, BINA
[unreadable text] (*Sa-ra-na-tha*)
Bho-pal
Bhom-bhe
Man-di
Man-mad
Manikapur, MANIKAPUR
Mu-dzu-phar-pur
Me-dha-ra-si, MADRAS
Mya-ngan-med-kyi mChod-rten
rTswa-mchog-grong (Ma-tha-kowar)
mTsho Padma (Ro-war-sar)
Dzalandhara, JALLANDAR
Waranāsi (Binrasi)
Rag-sol, Bal-yul la 'gro-sa
Rameshwar, 'dir Singgalar nye
Rawal-pindi, RAWALPINDI
Shar rTswa-mchog-grong (Mahāmuni)
Shikohabad, SHIKOHABAD

San-ci
Sani-pur, SANPUR
Si-go-li
Siligori
Sil-tan-gan-ji
Sultan-pur
Ser-skya (Kapilabastu)
La-hor
Lag-no'u
Limbini (Ru-min-de)
Lu-na-ba-la
lHa-babs-gnas (Sang-khi-sa)
lHo-phyogs dPal-gyi-ri, Na-gar-ji-na-kon-ṭa
Ag-ra
A-jan-ta
Am-'bar-sar
Am-ba-la, AMBALA
A'orang-ga-bad
A-la-ha-ba-da
Un-ri-har, Aun-rihar
E-lo-ra
Otantapuri (Biharsharib)
Otibisha (Puri)

Bibliography

Tibetan Sources

Note: Authors and abbreviations are listed in Tibetan alphabetical order.

Kirti, sPrul-sku (20th cent.). 1983. *dGe 'dun chos 'phel gyi rab byed*. Dharamsala, Library of Tibetan Works & Archives.

dKar-chag = Jampa Samten Shastri (compiler). 1983. *Catalogue of the Library of Tibetan Works and Archives* (*Manuscript Section*), vol.1, *Historial Works* (*Bod kyi dpe mdzod khang gi bod yig phyag dpe'i dkar chag*, deb dang-po, *rGyal-rabs sogs lo rgyus kyi skor*). Dharamsala, Library of Tibetan Works & Archives.

Khang-dkar, Tshul-khrims sKal-bzang (20th cent.). 1992. "dGe bshes shes rabs dang dge 'dun chos 'phel", In *Tibetan Studies. Proceedings of the 6th Seminar of the International Association for Tibetan Studies, Fagernes 1992*, vol.1. (Ed.) P. Kvaerne, Oslo, The Institute for Comparative Research in Human Culture, pp.430-440.

dGe-'dun Chos-'phel (1903-1951). (*alias* Drang-po Dharma). 1938. " 'Jig rten ril mo 'am zlum po?" *Melong*, 10 (7-8), 28 June, p.11.

dGe 'dun Chos 'phel. 1950. *rGya gar gyi gnas chen khag la 'grod pa'i lam yig*. Gangtok, Sikkim Government Press.

dGe 'dun Chos 'phel. 1968. *rGya gar gyi gnas chen khag la bgrod pa'i lam yig. Guide to Buddhist Sacred Places in India*. Dalhousie, Ḍa-hor Blo[-bzang] Rab[-rgyas].

dGe-'dun Chos-'phel. 1976. *rGya gar gyi gnas chen khag la bgrod pa'i lam yig / dge 'dun chos 'phel gyis mdzad pa'o // Guide to Buddhist Sacred Places in India by dGe 'dun chos 'phel.* New Delhi, Tre-hor gDong-thog bsTan-pa'i rGyal-mtshan.

dGe-'dun Chos-'phel. 1984. *rGya gar gnas chen khag la bgrod pa'i lam yig mdo smad pa dge 'dun chos 'phel nas brtsams pa bzhugs so //. A Guide Book to the Holy Places of India by Amdowa Gendun Chhephel.* Sarnath, Sushil Printing Press.

dGe-'dun Chos-'phel. 1985. *Dhammapada* (*Chos kyi tshigs su bcad pa*). Berkeley, Dharma Publishing.

dGe-'dun Chos-'phel. 1986. *mKhas dbang dge 'dun chos 'phel gyis mdzad pa'i gtam rgyud gser gyi thang ma (gTam-rGyud-gSer-Gyi-Thaṅ-Ma of dGe-hDun-Chos-hPhel With an Introduction cum Review by Ven. S. Rinpoche*. (Zhu-sgrig-pa) Blo-bzang Nor-bu Shāstrī, Sarnath, Central Institute of Higher Tibetan Studies (Dalai Lama Tibeto-Indologcal Series—VII).

dGe-'dun Chos-'phel. 1989. *rGya gar gyi gnas chen khag la bgrod pa'i lam yig bzhugs so*. In: *Mkhas dbang dge 'dun chos 'phel gyi gsung rtsom phyogs sgrig*. Chengdu, Si-khron Mi-rigs dPe-skrun-khang, 1989, pp.351-395.

dGe-'dun Chos-'phel. 1990. *rGya gar gyi gnas chen khag la bgrod pa'i lam yig bzhugs so*. In: *dGe 'dun chos 'phel gyi gsung rtsom*, vol. 3. (Comp. & Ed.) Hor-khang bSod-nams dPal-'bar, Lhasa, Bod-ljongs Bod-yig dPe-rnying dPe-skrun-khang (Gangs-can Rig-mdzod, 12), pp.311-351.

dGe-'dun Chos-'phel. 1990a. *Bod chen po'i srid lugs dang 'brel ba'i rgyal rabs deb ther dkar po*. In *dGe 'dun chos 'phel gyi gsung rtsom*, vol. 3. (Comp. & Ed.) Hor-khang bSod-nams dPal-'bar, et al., Lhasa, Bod-ljongs Bod-yig dPe-rnying dPe-skrun-khang (Gangs-can Rig-mdzod, 12), pp.205-300.

dGe-'dun Chos-'phel. 1990b. *'Phags pa gnas brtan pa rnams kyi mdo sde snod bsdus pa las / phan tshigs kyi mdo phran gnyis pa chos kyi tshigs su bcas pa*. In *dGe 'dun chos 'phel gyi gsung rtsom*, vol.2. (Comp. & Ed.) Hor-khang bSod-nams dPal-'bar, *et al*., Lhasa, Bod-ljongs Bod-yig dPe-rnying dPe-skrun-khang (Gangs-can Rig-mdzod, 11), pp.193-270.

dGe-'dun Chos-'phel. 1998. *rGya gar gnas yig bdus pa*. In: *Gnas yig phyogs bsgrigs*. (Eds.) dGe-'dun Chos-'phel, *et. al*. Chengdu, Si-khron Mi-rigs dPe-skrun-khang, 1998, pp.340-382.

'Gos Lo-tsā-ba, gZhon-nu-dpal (1392-1481). 1984. *Deb ther sngon po*, 2 Vols. Chengdu, Si-khron Mi-rigs dPe-skrun-khang.

Champa Thupten Zongtse (=rDzong-rtse Byams-pa Thub-bstan, 20th cent.). 1981. *The Biography of Chag Lo-tsā-ba Chos rje dpal (Dharmasvāmin) by Śākya'i dge bsñen chos dpal dar dpyaṅ*. New Delhi, International Academy of Indian Culture (Śata-Piṭaka Series, 266).

'Jam-dbyangs mKhyen-brtse'i dBang-po (1820-1892). 1977. *'Jam dpal sgyu 'phrul dra ba'i rgyud la brten nas sgrub brgyud shing rta brgyad kyi lam srol 'chad tshul dang zin bris skor sna tshogs*. In *The Collected Works of the Great 'Jam dbyaṅs Mkhyen brtse'i dbang po*, vol.3 (Ga). Gangtok, Gonpo Tseten, pp.1-735.

gTam-rgyud = dGe 'dun Chos 'phel. 1990. *rGyal khams rig pas bskor ba'i gtam rgyud gser gyi thang ma*. In *dGe 'dun chos 'phel gyi gsung rtsom*, vols. 1-2. (Comp.) Hor-khang bSod-nams dPal-'bar, *et al.*, Lhasa, (Gangs-can Rig-mdzod, 10), pp.3-426, (Gangs-can Rig-mdzod, 11), pp.3-188.

rTa-tshag Tshe-dbang-rgyal (active mid-15th cent.). 1994. *Dam pa'i chos kyi byung ba'i legs bshad lho rong chos 'byung ngam rta tshag chos 'byung zhes rtsom pa'i yul ming du chags pa'i ngo mtshar zhing dkon pa'i dpe khyad par can.* Xining, Bod-ljongs Bod-yig dPe-rnying dPe-skrun-khang.

rDo-rje-rgyal (20th cent.). 1997. " 'Dzam gling rig pa'i dpa' bo rdo brag dge 'dun chos 'phel gyi byung ba brjod pa bden gtam rna ba'i bcud len", In *dGe 'dun chos 'phel.* N.p., Kan-su'u Mi-rigs dPe-skrun-khang, pp.1-152.

Nor-brang O-rgyan (20th cent). 1995. "Bod kyi grags can rtsom pa po ngo sprod: dge 'dun chos 'phel", *Bod kyi rtsom rig sgyu rtsal*, 3, pp.75-77.

rNam-thar = Mi-pham dGe-legs rNam-par rGyal-ba'i lha. N.d. *rJe btsun grub pa'i dbang phyug dam pa dpag bsam ye shes zhabs kyi rnam par thar pa mchog gi spyod tshul rgya mtsho'i snying po*. Typescript transcription of 67 folio xylograph from the Mang-yul Ri-rgyal dPal-'bar blocks, private collection of E. Gene Smith.

rNam-bshad = Blo-bzang dPal-ldan Ye-shes, Third Paṇ-chen Bla-ma (1739-1780). 1775. *Grub pa'i gnas chen po shambhala'i rnam bshad 'phags yul gyi rtogs brjod dang bcas pa ngo mtshar bye ba'i 'byung gnas*. In *rJe btsun blo bzang dpal ldan ye shes dpal bzang po'i gsung 'bum*, vol.Nya. Beijing, xylographic edition of the 1980s, ff.683-781 (=1a-50a).

Phun-tshogs. 1998. *dGe bshes shes rab rgya mtsho dang rdo sbis grwa tshang*. Beijing, Mi-rigs dPe-skrun-khang.

Bu-ston, Rin-chen-grub (1290-1364). 1966. *bDe mchog [nyung ngu'i rgyud kyi] spyi rnam don gsal*, In *The Collected Works of Bu-ston*, Part 6 (Cha). (Ed.) Lokesh Chandra, New Delhi, International Academy of Indian Culture, pp.1-118.

Bod-rgya = Bod rgya tshig mdzod chen mo, 3 vols. Beijing, Mi-rigs dPe-skrun-khang, 1986.

Bla-chung A-pho, Shes-rab rGya-mtsho (1905-1975). 1973. Untitled Tibetan entry In *Biographical Dictionary of Tibet and Tibetan Buddhism*, vol.4. (Ed. & Comp.) Lama Khetsun Sangpo, Delhi, pp.634-657.

bTsan-po No-mon-han, 'Jam-dpal Chos-kyi bsTan-'dzin 'Phrin-las (1789-1838). 1980. *'Dzam gliṅ rgyas par bśad pa thag riṅ gsal bar mthoṅ byed dur ba na* or *'Dzam gliṅ chen po'i rgyas bśad snod bcud kun gsal me loṅ. The rare 1830 redaction of the monumental Tibetan work on the geography of the world.* New Delhi, Ngawang Sopa.

[gZhis-rtse] Ri-kha, Blo-bzang bsTan-'dzin (20th cent.). 1972. "mDo smad yi mkhas pa dge 'dun chos 'phel", In *rGyun mkho'i chos srid shes bya gnas tshul*. Varanasi, Legs-bshad gTer-mdzod-khang, pp.173-187.

gZhis-rtse Ri-kha, Blo-bzang bsTan-'dzin (20th cent.). 1985. *rGya gar nang pa'i gnas chen khag gi gnas yig*. New Delhi, Ri-kha Khyim-tshang.

Zam-gdong-pa, Blo-bzang bsTan-'dzin (20th cent.). 1986. "Introduction cum Review", In *gTam-rGyud-gSer Gyi-Thaṅ-Ma of dGe-hDun-Chos-hPhel*. Sarnarth, Central Institute of Higher Tibetan Studies, pp.1-27.

Rak-ra sPrul-sku, bKras-mthong Thub-bstan Chos-dar (20th cent.). 1980. *dGe 'dun chos 'phel gyi lo rgyus*. Dharamsala, Library of Tibetan Works and Archives.

Ri-pa Karma Bag-yod, Seventh (1876-1942). 1994. *Collected Writings of the VIIth Ripa Karma Bag-Yod, Karma sgrub brgyud 'phrin las rab rgyas dpal bzaṅ po* (1876-1942). Kollegal, Ripa Bag-yod Rinpoche.

Shes-rab rGya-mtsho (c.1884-1968). 1984. *Klu sgrub dgongs rgyan la che long du brtags pa mi 'jigs sengge'i nga ro*, In *rJe btsun shes rab rgya mtsho 'jam dpal dgyes pa'i blo gros kyi gsung rtsom*, vol.3. Xining, mTsho-sngon Mi-rigs dPe-skrun-khang, pp.1-246.

Hor-khang, bSod-nams dPal-'bar (20th cent.). 1983. "mKhas dbang dge 'dun chos 'phel gyi rtogs pa brjod pa dag pa'i snang ba", *Bod ljong zhib 'jug*, 2, pp.3-31.

Hor-khang, bSod-nams dPal-'bar (Ed. & Comp.). 1990. *dGe 'dun chos 'phel gyi gsung rtsom*, 3 vols. Lhasa, Bod-ljongs Bod-yig dPe-rnying dPe-skrun-khang (Gangs-can Rig-mdzod 10-12).

Sources in Other Languages

Anon (=Anonymous). 1898a. "A Visit to the Lumbini Garden and Kapilavastu", *Journal of the Maha-Bodhi Society*, 7:3, pp.24-28; 7:5, pp.45-47.

Anon. 1898b. "The Great Chinese Traveller, VIII", *Journal of the Maha-Bodhi Society*, 7:1, pp.2-3; 7:7, pp.59-60.

Anon. 1899. "Rajgriha or Rajgir", *Journal of the Maha-Bodhi Society*, 7:9, pp.87-88.

Anon. 1917. "Hiuen Tsiang-The Chinese Monk-Pilgrim", *The Maha-Bodhi and the United Buddhist World*, 25:11, pp.248-258.

Anon. 1920. "The Enshrinement of the Holy Relic of the Blessed One in the New Sri Dharma Rajika Chaitya Vihara in Calcutta", *The Maha-Bodhi and the United Buddhist World*, 28:12, pp.257-261.

Anon. 1928. "Buddhist Pilgrim's Railway Guide Map", *Buddhist India*, September (Third Quarter), p.230.

Anon. 1930. "Discovery of Buddha Relics. Remains of Great Stupa in Madras Presidency", *The Maha-Bodhi. Journal of the Maha Bodhi Society*, 38:3, pp.126-128.

Anon. 1931. *The Maha-Bodhi. Journal of the Maha Bodhi Society. Mulagandhakuti Vihara Inauguration Number*, 39:11-12.

Anon. 1932. "The First Anniversary of the Mulagandhakuti Vihara", *The Maha-Bodhi. Journal of the Maha Bodhi Society*, 40:11, p.1.

Anon. 1933. "A Detailed Account of the Anniversary Celebration at Sarnath", *The Maha-Bodhi. Journal of the Maha Bodhi Society*, 41:1-2, pp.38-41.

Anon. 1937. "Opening of the Dharamsala at Sarnath", *The Maha-Bodhi. Journal of the Maha Bodhi Society*, 45:2, pp.80-83.

Anon. 1941. "Lama Geshe Chompell", *The Maha-Bodhi. Journal of the Maha Bodhi Society*, 49:8, pp.291-295.

Aris, M. 1979. *Bhutan. The Early History of a Himalayan Kingdom*. Warminster, Aris & Phillips.

Aris, M. 1986. *Sources for the History of Bhutan*. Wien, Arbeitskreis für Tibetische und Buddhistische Studien Universität Wien, (Wiener Studien zur Tibetologie und Buddhismuskunde, Heft 14).

Aris, M. 1995. *'Jigs-med-gling-pa's "Discourse on India" of 1789. A Critical Edition and Annotated Translation of the lHo-phyogs rgya-gar-gyi gtam brtag-pa brgyad-kyi me-long*. Tokyo, International Institute of Buddhist Studies of International College for Advanced Buddhist Studies (Studia Philologica Buddhica, Occasional Paper Series, IX).

Bacot, J. 1914. "Drimed Kundan, Une version tibétaine dialoguée du Vessantara Jātaka", *Journal Asiatique*, 14, pp.221-305.

Barua, B. 1931-1934. *Gayā and Buddha-Gayā: early history of the holy land*, 2 vols. Calcutta, C. Chatterjee.

Barua, D.K. 1969. *Vihāras in Ancient India*. Calcutta, Indian Publications.

Beal, S. 1884. *Si-yu-ki Buddhist Records of the Western World*. London, Kegan Paul, Trench, Trübner & Co. Ltd.

Bechert, H. 1966. *Buddhismus, Staat und Gesellschaft in den Ländern des Theravāda-Buddhismus*, Band 1. Frankfurt/ Berlin, Metzner.

Bechert, H. 1984. "Buddhist Revival in East and West", In *The World of Buddhism*. (Eds.) H. Bechert & R. Gombrich, London, Thames & Hudson Ltd., pp.273-285.

Berry, S. 1995. *Monks, Spies and a Solidier of Fortune. The Japanese in Tibet*. London, Athlone.

Bharati, A. 1978. "Actual and Ideal Himalayas: Hindu Views of the Mountains", In *Himalayan Anthropology: The Indo-Tibetan Interface*. (Ed.) J. Fisher, The Hague, Mouton, pp.77-82.

Blakiston, J.F. 1935. "Address on the Occasion of the Presentation of Buddhist Relics to the Maha Bodhi Society at Sarnath on the 10th November, 1935", *The Maha-Bodhi. Journal of the Maha Bodhi Society*, 43:12, pp.563-566.

Bogin, B. & H. Decleer. 1997. "Who was "this evil friend" ("the dog", the "fool", "the tyrant") in Gedün Chöphel's Sad Song?", *The Tibet Journal*, 22:3, pp.67-78.

Brough, J. 1948. "Legends of Khotan and Nepal", *Bulletin of the School of Oriental and African Studies*, 12, pp.333-339.

Broughton, B.L. 1931. "Buddhist Pilgrimage", *The Maha-Bodhi. Journal of the Maha Bodhi Society*, 39:5-6, pp.216-233; 39:7, pp.298-309; 39:8, pp.352-364; 39:9, pp.421-429.

Byron, R. 1933. *First Russia, Then Tibet*. London, Macmillan & Co. Ltd.

Chakrabarti, D.K. 1988. *A History of Indian Archaeology from the beginning to 1947*. New Delhi, Munshiram Manoharlal.

Chandrima, Phra Maha. 1902. "Guide to the Sacred Sites of the Buddhist Holy Land", *The Maha-Bodhi and the United Buddhist World*.

Combe, G.A. 1926. *A Tibetan on Tibet*. London, T. Fisher Unwin Ltd.

Cunningham, A. 1871. *Archaeological Survey of India. Four reports made during the years 1862-63-64-65*. Delhi, Indological Book House (reprint 1972).

Cunningham, A. 1892. *Mahābodhi or the Great Buddhist Temple under the Bodhi Tree at Buddha-gaya*. London, W.H. Allen & Co.

Das, S.C. 1902. *Tibetan-English Dictionary*. Calcutta, Bengal Secretariat Book Depot.

David-Neel, A. 1983. *My Journey to Lhasa*. London, Virago.

Daya Ram Sahni. 1933. "Presentation of a Buddhist Relic to the Mahabodhi Society", *The Maha-Bodhi. Journal of the Maha Bodhi Society*, 41:1-2:, p.1-4.

Daya Ram Sahni. 1936. "The Eight Great Places of Buddhist Pilgrimage", *The Maha-Bodhi. Journal of the Maha Bodhi Society*, 44:4, pp.152-161.

Decleer, H. 1998. "Review Article: *Tibetan Literature: Studies in Genre. Essays in Honor of Geshe Lhundrup Sopa*", *The Tibet Journal*, 23:1, pp.67-106.

Dejin Zangmo (= H. Stoddard). 1978. "More on Gedun Choephel", *Tibetan Review*, 13 (December), pp.21-22.

Dharmapala, Anagarika. 1908. *Buddha Gaya*. Calcutta, Maha Bodhi Society.

Dharmapala, Anagarika. 1923a. "The Temple at Bodh-Gaya", *The Maha-Bodhi and the United Buddhist World*, 31:2, pp.56-64.

Dharmapala, Anagarika. 1923b. *History of the Buddha Gaya Temple*. Calcutta, Maha Bodhi Society.

Dharmapala, Anagarika. 1965. *Return to Righteousness. A Collection of Speeches, Essays and Letters of the Anagarika Dharmapala*. (Ed.) A. Guruge, Colombo, The Government Press.

Dhondup, K. 1978. "Gedun Chophel: the Man Behind the Legend", *Tibetan Review*, October, pp.10-18.

Dhondup, K. (trans.). 1983. "The Evolution of *U'med* from *U'chen* script", *The Tibet Journal*, 8:1, pp.56-7.

Ehrhard, F.-K. 1991. "Further Renovations of Svayambhunath (from the 13th to the 17th centuries)", *Ancient Nepal*, 123-125 (April-Sept.), pp.10-20.

Goldstein, M.C. 1989. *A History of Modern Tibet, 1913-1951. The demise of the Lamaist State*. Berkeley, University of California Press.

Gombrich, R. 1988. *Theravāda Buddhism. A social history from Benares to modern Colombo*. London, Routledge & Kegan Paul.

Gombrich, R. & G. Obeyesekere. 1988. *Buddhism Transformed. Religious Change in Sri Lanka*. Princeton, Princeton University Press.

Gunavardhana, T. 1930. "My Trip to India", *The Maha-Bodhi. Journal of the Maha Bodhi Society*, 38:1, pp.6-16.

Guy, J. 1991. "The Mahābodhi temple: pilgrim souvenirs of Buddhist India", *The Burlington Magazine*, 133, pp.356-368.

Härtel, H. 1991. "Archaeological Research on Ancient Buddhist Sites", In *The Dating of the Historical Buddha*, Part 1. (Ed.) H. Bechert, Göttingen, Vandenhoeck & Ruprecht (Abhandlungen der Akademie der Wissenschaften in Göttingen, Philologisch-Historische Klasse, Dritte Folge Nr.189), pp.61-89.

Havnevik, H. 1999. *The Life of Jetsun Lochen Rinpoche (1865-1951) As Told in Her Autobiography*. Unpublished doctoral dissertation, University of Oslo, Oslo.

Hecker, H. 1993. *Dhammapada. Ein bibliographischer Fürer durch Übersetzungen der berühmtesten buddhistischen Spruchsammlung*. Konstanz, Universität Konstanz (Forschungsprojekt Buddhistischer Modernismus, Forschungsberichte 7).

Hewavitarane, C.A. 1936. "Ancient Buddhist Sites in India", *The Maha-Bodhi. Journal of the Maha Bodhi Society*, 44:1, pp.31-37.

von Hinüber, O. 1989. "Buddhistische Kultur in Zentralasien und Afghanistan", In *Der Buddhismus, Geschichte und Gegenwart*. (Eds.) H. Bechert & R. Gombrich, München, C.H. Beck, pp.108-122.

Hopkins, J. & D.Y. Yuthok. 1992. *Tibetan Arts of Love*. Ithaca, Snow Lion Publications.

Huber, T. 1990. "Where Exactly Are Cāritra, Devikoṭa and Himavat? A Sacred Geography Controversy and the Development of Tantric Buddhist Pilgrimage Sites in Tibet", *Kailash. A Journal of Himalayan Studies*, 16:3-4, pp.121-65.

Huber T. 1997. "Colonial Archaeology, International Missionary Buddhism and the First Example of Modern Tibetan Literature", In *Bauddhavidyāsudhākaraḥ: Studies in Honour of Heinz Bechert on the Occasion of His 65th Birthday*. (Eds.) Petra Kieffer-Pülz & Jens-Uwe Hartmann, Swisttal-Odendorf, Indica et Tibetica Verlag, (Indica et Tibetica, 30), pp. 297-318.

Huber, T. Forthcoming. *The Holy Land Reborn. Pilgrimage and the Reinvention of Buddhist India in the Tibetan Tradition.*

Hultzsch, E. 1969. *Inscriptions of Asoka*. Delhi, Indological Book House (reprint edition).

Huntington, S.L. & J.C. Huntington. 1990. *Leaves from the Bodhi Tree: The Art of Pāla India (8th-12th centuries) and Its International Legacy*. Seattle/London, Dayton Art Institute/University of Washington Press.

Jackson, D. 1989. *The 'Miscellaneous Series' of Tibetan Texts in the Bihar Research Society, Patna: A Handlist*. Stuttgart, Franz Steiner Verlag (Tibetan and Indo-Tibetan Studies, 2).

Karmay, H. (=H. Stoddard). 1980. "dGe-'dun Chos-'phel the Artist", In *Tibetan Studies in Honour of Hugh Richardson.*

Aris, M. & Aung San Suu Kyi (Eds.), Warminster, Aris & Phillips, pp.145-149.

Kawasaki, S. 1992. "Discrepancies in the Sanskrit and Tibetan Texts of Bhavya's *Madhyamaka-hṛdaya-Tarkajvālā* (the IXth and Xth Chapters", In *Tibetan Studies. Proceedings of the 5th Seminar of the International Association of Tibetan Studies, NARITA 1989*, vol.1. (Eds.) Ihara Shōren & Yamaguchi Zuihō, Narita, Naritasan Shinshoji, pp.130-143.

van der Kuijp, L.W.J. 1996. "Tibetan Historiography", In *Tibetan Literature. Studies in Genre*. (Eds.) J.I. Cabezón & R.R. Jackson, Ithaca, Snow Lion, pp.39-56.

Kvaerne, P. 1998. "Khyung-sprul 'Jigs-med nam-mkha'i rdo-rje (1897-1955): An Early Twentieth-century Tibetan Pilgrim in India", In *Pilgrimage in Tibet.* (Ed.) A. McKay, Richmond, Curzon Press, pp.71-84.

Lama Chimpa & A. Chattopadhyaya. 1970. *Tāranātha's History of Buddhism in India*. Simla, Indian Institute of Advanced Study.

Lama Geshe Chömphel (=dGe-'dun Chos-'phel). 1941. "Two Famous Bengali Pandits in Tibet", *The Maha-Bodhi. Journal of the Maha Bodhi Society*, 49:1, pp.31-32.

Lamotte, E. 1988. *History of Indian Buddhism from the Origins of the Śaka Era*. Translated by S. Webb-Boin. Louvain-la-neuve, Institut Orientaliste de l'Université Catholique de Louvain.

Large-Blondeau, A.M. 1960. "Les pèlerinages tibétains", In *Les Pèlerinages*. Paris, Editions du Seuil, pp.199-246 (Collection Sources Orientale, 3).

Legge, J. 1886. *A Record of Buddhistic Kingdoms*. Oxford, Clarendon Press.

Leidy, D.P. & R.A.F. Thurman. 1997. *Mandala. The Architecture of Enlightenment*. London, Thames & Hudson.

Leoshko, J. (Ed.). 1988. *Bodhgaya the Site of Enlightenment*. Bombay, Marg Publications.

Lhalungpa, L.P. 1977. *The Life of Milarepa*. New York, E.P. Dutton.

Longhurst, A.H. 1931. "Excavations at Nāgārjunikonda", *Archaeological Survey of India, Annual Reports, 1927-1928*, pp.113-121.

Longhurst, A.H. 1933. "Excavations at Nāgārjunikonda", *Archaeological Survey of India, Annual Reports, 1928-1929*, pp.100-104.

Longhurst, A.H. 1935. "Excavations at Nāgārjunikonda", *Archaeological Survey of India, Annual Reports, 1929-1930*, pp.144-151.

Lopez, Jr., D. 1994a. "dGe 'dun chos 'phel's *Klu sgrub dgongs rgyan*: a preliminary study", In *Tibetan Studies. Proceedings of the 6th Seminar of the International Association for Tibetan Studies, Fagernes 1992*, vol.1. (Ed.) P. Kvaerne, Oslo, The Institute for Comparative Research in Human Culture, pp.491-500.

Lopez, Jr., D. 1994b. "dGe 'dun Chos 'phel's Position on *Vigrahavyāvartinī* 29", In *The Buddhist Forum, volume III 1991-1993. Papers in honour and appreciation of Professor David Seyfort Ruegg's contribution to Indological, Buddhist and Tibetan Studies.* (Eds.) T. Skorupski & U. Pagel, London, School of Oriental and African Studies University of London, pp.161-184.

Lopez, Jr., D. 1995. "Madhyamika Meets Modernity: The Life and Works of Gedun Chopel", *Tricycle*, Spring, pp.42-51.

Macdonald, A. 1970. "Le Dhānyakaṭaka de Man-luṅs Guru", *Bulletin de l'École Française d'Extrême-Orient*, 57, pp.169-213.

Macdonald, A.W. 1985. "Points of View on Halase, a holy place in East Nepal", *The Tibet Journal*, 10:3, pp.1-13.

Macdonald, A.W. & Dvags-po Rin-po-che. 1981. "Un guide peu lu des lieux-saints du Népal - II eme Partie", In *Tantric and Taoist Studies in honour of R.A. Stein*, vol.1. (Ed.) M. Strickmann, Bruxelles, Institut Belge des Hautes Etudes Chinoises, pp.237-273.

Mengele, I. 1999. *dGe-'dun-chos-'phel. A Biography of the 20th Century Tibetan Scholar*. Dharamsala, Library of Tibetan Works and Archives.

Monier-Williams, M. 1899. *A Sanskrit-English Dictionary*. Oxford, Oxford University Press.

Nakamura, H. 1980. "The Aṣṭamahāsthānacaityastotra and the Chinese and Tibetan versions of a text similar to it", In *Indianisme et bouddhisme. Mélanges offerts à Mgr Étienne Lamotte*. Louvain-la-neuve, Institut Orientaliste de l'Université Catholique de Louvain, pp.259-265.

Nālandā Translation Committee. 1982. *The Life of Marpa The Translator*. Boulder, Shambhala.

Naojiro Kitamura. 1899. "Life of Fa-Hian", *Journal of the Maha-Bodhi Society*, 8:73, pp.64-67.

Narain, S. 1930. "Chinese Pilgrims", *The Maha-Bodhi. Journal of the Maha Bodhi Society*, 38:1, pp.28-31.

Narain, S. 1932. "Opening Ceremony of Mulagandhakuti Vihara (Sarnath)", *The Buddhist*, 3:1 (new series), pp.9-12.

Narain, S. 1934. "The Travels of Fa-Hsien (399-414 A.D.)",

The Maha-Bodhi. Journal of the Maha Bodhi Society, 42:8, pp.354-358.

Narain, S. 1937. *Sarnath*. Calcutta, Maha Bodhi Society (Maha Bodhi Pamphlet Series, 10).

Narkyid, N. 1982. "In Defence of Amdo Gendun Chomphel's Theory of the Origin of the Tibetan Script", *The Tibet Journal*, 7:3, pp.23-34.

National Atlas of India, 2 vols. Calcutta, Government of India, 1979.

Nietupski, P.K. 1999. *Labrang. A Tibetan Buddhist Monastery at the Crossroads of Four Civilizations*. Ithaca, Snow Lion Publications.

Norboo, S. 1978. *The White Annals*. Dharamsala, Library of Tibetan Works & Archives.

Obermiller, E. 1932. *History of Buddhism (Chos-hbyung) by Bu-ston, II Part. The History of Buddhism in India and Tibet*. Heidelberg, Harrassowitz (Materialien zur Kunde des Buddhismus, 19).

Oldham, C.E.A.W. 1937. "Some Remarks on the Models of the Bodh Gayā Temple Found at Nar-Thang," *Journal of the Bihar and Orrisa Research Society*, 23:4, pp.418-428.

Pema Dorjee. 1996. *Stūpa and Its Technology: A Tibeto-Buddhist Perspective*. New Delhi, Indra Gandhi National Centre for the Arts.

Rakra Thetong. 1992. "Gendun Choephel ou la perte d'un savant", *Lungta*, 6, pp.19-23.

Ramble, C. 1999. "Gaining Ground: Representations of Territory in Bon and Tibetan Popular Tradition", In *Sacred Spaces and Powerful places in Tibetan Culture: A Collection of Essays*. (Ed.) T. Huber, Dharamsala, Library of Tibetan Works and Archives, pp.3-33.

Rea, A. 1894. *South Indian Buddhist Antiquities*. Madras, Government Press.

Ricca, F. & E. Lo Bue. 1993. *The Great Stupa of Gyantse. A Complete Pantheon of the Fifteenth Century*. London, Serindia.

Richardson, H.E. 1978. "Review Article: Gedun Chophel's "Unfinished" The White Annals (Deb-ther dKar-po)", *Tibetan Review*, October, pp.19-22.

Rispaud, J. 1966. "Contribution à la Géograpie Historique de la Haute Birmanie (Mien, Pong, Kośambī et Kamboja)", In *Essays Offered to G.H. Luce by His Colleagues and Friends in Honor of His Seventy-Fifth Birthday*, vol.1. (Eds.) Ba Shin, J. Boisselier & A.B. Griswold, Ascona, Artibus Asiae, pp.213-223.

Robinson, R.H. & W.L. Johnson. 1997. *The Buddhist Religion. A Historical Introduction*, 4th edition. Belmont, Wadsworth Publishing Co.

Roerich, G. 1959. *Biography of Dharmasvāmin* (*Chag lo tsaba Chos-rje-dpal*) *A Tibetan Monk Pilgrim*. Patna, K.P. Jayaswal Research Institute.

Roerich, G. 1976. *The Blue Annals*, 2nd edition. Delhi, Motilal Banarsidass.

Rowland, Jr., B. 1938. "A Miniature replica of the Mahābodhi temple," *Journal of the Indian Society of Oriental Art*, 5, pp.73-83.

Ruegg, D.S. 1989. "A Tibetan's Odyssey: A Review Article", *Journal of the Royal Asiatic Society*, 2, pp.304-311.

Saddhananda, Bhikshu N. 1898. "A Visit to Kapilavastu", *Journal of the Maha-Bodhi Society*, 7:1, pp.7-8.

Sanderson, A. 1990. "Evidence of the Textual Dependence of the Buddhist Yogānuttaratantras on the Tantric Śaiva Canon", unpublished manuscript of seminar delivered at Universität Hamburg, May 1990.

Sanderson, A. 1994. "Vajrayāna: Origin and Function", In *Buddhism Into the Year 2000: International Conference Proceedings*. Bangkok & Los Angeles, The Dhammakaya Foundation, pp.87-102.

Sankrityayan, R. 1937. "Second Search of Sanskrit Palm-Leaf Mss. in Tibet", *Journal of the Bihar and Orrisa Research Society*, 23:1, pp.1-57.

Schubert, J. 1935a. "Der tibetische Māhātmya des Wallfahrtsplatzes Triloknāth", *Artibus Asiae*, 5:fasc.1, pp.76-78; fasc. 2-4, pp.127-136.

Schubert, J. 1935b. "Tibetische Literatur in modernem Gewande (Mit einem Exkurs über tibetische Zeitungen)", *Artibus Asiae*, 5:fasc.1, pp.95-98.

Siiger, H. 1951. "Dancing Pilgrims from Tibet", *Geografisk Tidsskrift*, 51, pp.1-26.

Siriwardhana, P.P. 1933. "Rewalsar Lake and its Temples", *The Maha-Bodhi. Journal of the Maha Bodhi Society*, 41:12, pp.511-512.

Snellgrove, D.L. 1978. *The Image of the Buddha*. London, Serindia Publications.

Sorensen, P.K. 1994. *Tibetan Buddhist Historiography. The Mirror Illuminating the Royal Genealogies. An Annotated Translation of the XIVth Century Tibetan Chronicle: rGyal-rabs gsal-ba'i me-long*. Wiesbaden, Harrassowitz Verlag.

Stein, A. 1929. *On Alexander's track to the Indus*. London, Macmillan and Co. Ltd.

Stoddard, H. 1985a. *Le Mendiant de L'Amdo*. Paris, Société d'Ethnographie (Recherches sur la Haute Asie, 9).

Stoddard, H. 1985b. "dGe-'dun Chos-'phel: The Two Latest Versions of his Life Stories by Kirti Rinpoche and Hor-Khang bSod-nams dPal-'bar", *The Tibet Journal*, 10:1, pp.44-48.

Stoddard, H. 1988. "The Long Life of rDo-sbis dGe-bšes Šes-rab rGya-mcho", In *Tibetan Studies. Proceedings of the 4th Seminar of the International Association for Tibetan Studies Schloss Hohenkammer-Munich 1985*. (Eds.) H. Uebach & J. Panglung, München, Kommission für zentralasiatische Studien, Bayerische Akademie der Wissenschaften, pp.465-71.

Strong, J.S. 1995. *The Experience of Buddhism. Sources and Interpretations*. Belmont, Wadsworth Publishing Co.

Templeman, D. 1999. "Internal and External Geography in Spiritual Biography", In *Sacred Spaces and Powerful places in Tibetan Culture: A Collection of Essays*. (Ed.) T. Huber, Dharamsala, Library of Tibetan Works and Archives, pp.187-197.

Templeman, D. Forthcoming. *Tāranātha's life of Buddhguptanātha* (manuscript translation of *Grub chen buddha gupta'i rnam thar rje btsun nyid kyi zhal lung las gzhan du rang rtog gi dri mas ma sbags pa'i yi ge yang dag pa'o*, In: *The Collected Works of Jo-naṅ rJe-btsun Tāranātha*, vol.17. Leh, 1987, ff.532-575).

Thomas, F.W. 1935. *Tibetan Literary Texts and Documents Concerning Chinese Turkestan*, Part 1: Literary Texts. London, Royal Asiatic Society.

Tucci, G. 1931. "The Sea and Land Travels of a Buddhist Sādhu in the Sixteenth Century", *The Indian Historical Quarterly*, 7:4, pp.683-702.

Tucci, G. 1940. *Travels of Tibetan Pilgrims in the Swat Valley*. Calcutta, The Greater India Society.

Waddell, L.A. 1905. *Lhasa and Its Mysteries*. London, John Murray.

Waddell, L.A. 1934 [1894]. *The Buddhism of Tibet or Lamaism*, 2nd edition. Cambridge, W. Heffer & Sons.

Waldschmidt, E. 1951. *Das Mahāparinirvāṇasūtra. Teil III, Textbearbeitung: vorgang 33-51*. Berlin, Akademie-Verlag (Abhandlungen der Deutschen Akademie der Wissenschaften zu Berlin, Klasse für sprachen, Literatur und Kunst, Jahrgang 1950, Nr.3).

Weldon, D. & J.C. Singer. 1999. *The Sculptural Heritage of Tibet. Buddhist Art of the Nyingjei Lam Collection*. London, Laurence King.

Wylie, T.V. 1959. "A Standard System of Tibetan Transcription", *Harvard Journal of Asiatic Studies*, 2, pp.261-67.

Wylie, T.V. 1970. *A Tibetan Religious Geography of Nepal*. Roma, IsMEO (Serie Orientale Roma, XLII).

Index